YOUR NEXT MISSION:

A personal branding guide for the
military-to-civilian transition

LIDA CITROËN
Foreword by Dan Goldenberg, The Call of Duty Endowment

℗ Palisades Publishing

Palisades Publishing, Greenwood Village, Colorado
© 2014 by Lida Citroën. All rights reserved.
www.YourNextMissionBook.com

ISBN: 978-0-9831690-4-8
Library of Congress Control Number: 2013955006

Printed in the United States of America.
Edited by Ruth Goodman
Cover design and graphics by Scott Maiwald

ii

Dedicated to the parents who have supported their children in the Armed Forces--I cannot imagine what that experience was like for you.

To all the brave men and women who fought for our freedom, *thank you*. I enjoy the liberties of the American Dream because of your commitment, loyalty, and sacrifice.

Table of Contents

Acknowledgements

I find it difficult to possibly express in words my appreciation and acknowledgement for all of the people who helped make this project possible. With tremendous gratitude, I'll try.

John Jones, Staff Sergeant (Ret.) United States Marine Corps; Special Projects Director, Marine Corps Scholarship Fund. Thank you for giving me an opportunity to work with you back in 2009 and open the door fully to my ability to impact the transition of veterans across the United States. You took a chance on me (what could a civilian know about working with veterans?), and I hope I've lived up to your vision of where personal branding can impact returning service men and women.

Chris Ford, Lieutenant Colonel, United States Air Force. I cannot express how grateful I am for the contacts, feedback, and insights you provided to me on this book project. Your words and actions are consistent with your value as a leader and champion in the veteran reintegration space, and I am truly grateful to know you and call you a friend.

Katie Haddock, Colonel, United States Marine Corps; Executive Director, Wall Street Warfighters Foundation. Thank you for the access and opportunity to continue to serve the associates of the Wall Street Warfighters Foundation. What a blessing and an honor to be associated with this important mission!

Jon E. Arnold, Staff Sergeant, United States Army (Ret.); Advocate with The Army Wounded Warrior (AW2) Program, Warrior Transition Command. When we first met, I knew we'd get along great, Jon. While you root for the wrong football team, you are one of the most passionate veteran advocates I've had the pleasure to know. Thank you for your support and assistance in putting this book forward in a meaningful and relevant way.

Jerry Majetich, Staff Sergeant (Ret.) 304th Psychological Operations Company, United States Army; Vice President, Drexel Hamilton. There are few like you, Jerry—your spirit, energy, and optimism make you memorable. Your story makes you unique. You are not defined by circumstances and that lesson was critical to my understanding of how to address and add value to the wounded veteran returning to civilian life. Thank you for the gifts you shared with me and others.

John Melia, Corporal, United States Marine Corps.; 1st Lieutenant, United States Army National Guard; founder and former CEO, Wounded Warrior Project. I am so grateful to you for your insights, perspective, and contribution to this book, John. It is truly a pleasure and an honor to call you a friend and include your testimony in this message to veterans who will transition after you.

Denise Koster, Senior Talent Acquisition Specialist, Federal Reserve Bank of New York. As civilians, you and I share a passion for helping those who put their lives and families on the line to protect our freedoms. Thank you for your encouragement, feedback, and insights on this book, Denise. Your work is so important!

Lindsay Jefferson, Marketing Associate, LIDA360. I know none of this book would have come together as flawlessly as it has without your help and guidance, Lindsay. You are such an important part of my business and my life. We can both be so proud of this book!

Dan Goldenberg, Commander, United States Navy Reserve; Executive Director, The Call of Duty Endowment. Thank you for your important commitment and contribution to this book and the work of helping veterans gain opportunity through employment in the civilian sector. The work you are doing to fund worthy organizations will truly lift the resources needed to impact veteran transitions.

Kevin Preston, Colonel, United States Army (Ret.); Director of Veterans Initiatives at The Walt Disney Company; **James Rodriguez,** 1st Sergeant, United States Marine Corps (Ret.); Director, Government Relations, BAE Systems; and **Frank Clark,** Senior Master Sergeant, United States Air Force (Ret.); Director of Operations Support, USAA, thank you for spending so much time speaking with me about the intricacies and challenges of the military-to-civilian transition. Your advice and contributions are meaningful to those who come after you. You have truly paved the way to ensure veteran-friendly and veteran-committed organizations can thrive!

Paul Bogacz, Captain (Ret.), United States Air Force; Curriculum Developer, United States Personnel Professional Development School; **Dana Niemela,** Lieutenant, United States Navy; Program Manager, Homeless Veterans Reintegration Program at City and County of Denver; **Izzy Abbass,** Staff Sergeant, United States Army Reserve; Director of the Boots to Suits Program, University of Colorado Denver; past Commander, VFW Post 1; **Theresa Z. Blumberg,** Colonel, United

States Air Force Reserves (Ret.); Former Judge Advocate General and Chief of Joint Staff; Colorado National Guard; and Vice President and Co-Founder of Women Veterans of Colorado; **William Doe, III,** Lieutenant Colonel, United States Army (Ret.); **Matt McGuire,** Former United States Army SPC; **John R. Toth,** Lieutenant Colonel, United States Army (Ret.); **Jan Rutherford,** Special Forces medic; "A" team executive officer; a military intelligence officer; **Shane Schmutz,** Captain, United States Army; Executive Director, Veteran's Passport To Hope; and **Dick Young,** Rear Admiral United States Navy (Ret.), Colorado Chair, Employer Support of the Guard and Reserve, thank you from the bottom of my heart for your unwavering support, insights, feedback, and encouragement as I write this book and serve this great community!

Scott, Clark, and Beau. You are the three most important men in my life —always and forever. Thank you for your support as I took long trips away from home to work with veterans groups and counsel veterans just home from service. Thank you for giving me the time I needed to learn more and spend hours listening to veteran stories in order to gain the best practices and tools I needed to be effective in pursuing this passion for helping veterans. Without your encouragement and support this book could have remained just a dream.

As Nelson Mandela once said, *"There is no passion to be found playing small--in settling for a life that is less than the one you are capable of living."* I truly thank all of you who have been part of helping me share this important message with the brave men and women of our United States Armed Forces.

Foreword

Attending a military career fair a few months ago, a corporate recruiter introduced me to a young Navy officer preparing to leave the service. The recruiter didn't know what to make of him and thought I might be able to help. As I came to learn, he had said something very typical of veterans searching for their first civilian job: "I'll do anything." And as military veterans who are new to the civilian job search often do, he took a virtue of military service—a selfless, can-do attitude—and turned it into a sin of the civilian job search—telegraphing a lack of focus and unpreparedness. Recruiters are not career counselors—they have specific openings that must be filled by well-qualified candidates who can articulate their value in a compelling way.

In that innocent statement, a smart, experienced, energetic leader had taken himself out of contention for a job with a good company. And in fact, this is a very common occurrence among veterans, the first of many pitfalls a military member is likely to encounter in their initial civilian job search. Again and again, what seems to be the right thing to do in the military context—being humble, talking in terms of "we" instead of "I," and labeling extraordinary achievements as "just doing my job"—is exactly what not to when trying to get hired in the civilian world. While the experience of military service makes vets more successful once hired,[1] it does not prepare them to establish a "personal brand" that is so critical today in getting hired for the right position.

After getting to know Lida Citroën and her book, I'm confident she has created a guide to a rewarding career after military service. I was lucky enough to meet Lida through Lieutenant Colonel Chris Ford from the Warrior and Family Support Office of the Chairman of the Joint Chiefs of Staff. In a conversation with Chris, I remarked that vets could really use a comprehensive guide to getting hired, tailored for their unique needs— something that would stay with them beyond the required transition training we receive when exiting the service. Chris mentioned that he knew someone who was doing a wonderful job of creating just that: Lida Citroën.

Indeed, Lida has created a fantastic and accessible guide for driving success in a veteran's job search. Given her work helping many corporate business leaders create strong reputation management and personal branding strategies and the last four years customizing this work for veterans, she is uniquely qualified for the task. She has committed herself to sharing the same tips, resources, and techniques with veterans who, because of their service or background, do not have an understanding of or network into the corporate world.

Lida's message of personal branding helps place veterans on a more equal footing with their civilian counterparts. It's an approach that allows them to highlight their valuable and hard-won talents as leaders, technicians, and diligent contributors. These are attributes employers are

---

[1] Data from CEB's Corporate Leadership Council shows that veterans are 4% more productive and 3% more likely to be retained than their non-veteran peers.

seeking but also ones that vets have been stymied in communicating effectively to the market.

According to The Center for a New American Security's research, among the top six reasons companies do not hire vets are: "difficulty translating military skills into skills useful in the civilian workplace, a negative stereotype or negative attitude toward veterans, a mismatch between veterans' skills and those needed by companies, concern about subsequent deployments of guardsmen and reservists, the time veterans need to acclimate to the civilian environment and the difficulty in identifying veterans to hire."[2]

While many of these obstacles are based on employer ignorance, what's particularly wonderful about this book is that it arms a veteran with everything he or she needs to get past these barriers and advocate for themselves during the hiring process. Fundamentally, it shows them how to become more competitive and relevant so their value shines through and overcomes stereotypes an employer may hold.

At the time of this writing, veterans' unemployment in America remains a difficult issue to solve. Highly skilled, disciplined, and experienced post-9/11 veterans under age 30 are unemployed at twice the rate of their non-veteran peers.[3] My organization, The Call of Duty Endowment, attempts to address this problem by finding and funding the best non-profits at preparing veterans for their job search. The organizations we

---

[2] "Employing America's Veterans: Perspectives from Businesses," Margaret C. Harrell and Nancy Berglass, Center for New American Security, 2013.

[3] "The Employment Situation of Veterans," Syracuse University Institute for Veterans and Military Families, November 2013.

support are excellent at helping vets get on the path to career success, but given their high-touch model and limited resources, they can't reach every veteran in need. This book is a great way to support the unserved tens of thousands who desperately need help and focus in their career efforts.

Business professionals live in the world of differentiation, value propositions, and competitive advantage. Business schools and corporate experience teach civilian job seekers to capture the attention of target audiences with compelling and relevant messaging. At all levels of the civilian work environment, individuals are embracing the power of personal branding to cultivate a reputation that draws opportunities to them. Vets need to understand this too; that a strong personal brand gives them competitive advantage, connection with their passion, and a renewed sense of mission.

I hope the Navy vet I met a few months ago has landed a great job, but if he hasn't, I think this book would be of great value to him—in figuring out what he wants to do in the civilian world, translating his military achievements to skills necessary to compete for his dream job, and ultimately marketing these credentials through a compelling and focused personal brand. Lida Citroën has done a remarkable service for our veterans by putting this all together in a user-friendly manner. I hope you will unlock the value contained in this book and encourage other vets do the same. Good hunting!

-- Dan Goldenberg, The Call of Duty Endowment

Introduction

I met Jerry on my first day of a new workshop for veterans. I walked into the training room at Drexel Hamilton and was immediately greeted by a group of handsome, well-groomed, and very polite gentlemen. They were veterans who were going to listen to me teach them personal branding for the next three days. They seemed curious (maybe a bit skeptical), friendly, and professional.

One by one, I made my way around the room, meeting them and shaking hands. When I got to Jerry, he said, "I bet I'm the only person you'll meet today with plastic ears." I was taken aback. Jerry then extended a nub of a hand and I shook it. Jerry made an indelible impression on me that day—his confidence, authenticity, and smile made me comfortable and at ease.

In 2005, Al Qaeda had a bounty on Army Staff Sergeant Jerry Majetich's head, and the result of their focus led to an attack in Iraq, where Jerry's armored Humvee was attacked. Two artillery shells, bundled with 50 gallons of propane, took Jerry's vehicle from a safe transport to a crumbled mess of metal. Jerry sustained many wounds, spent years in the hospital, and had numerous surgeries to repair his burns and scars.

What the incident couldn't take away, however, was Jerry's infectious smile, his warm heart, and his passion for helping others. He was—and will always be—a leader and a fighter. That spirit can never be extinguished.

I have no direct connection to the military. No one in my immediate family has served in the armed forces, has paid the ultimate sacrifice first hand, or has welcomed home a soldier.

In 2009, my husband and I attended a Denver Broncos football game. It happened to be the game where they celebrated Veterans Day that year, and the team offered a tribute to our fallen heroes by including a touching speech by a recently returned soldier from Iraq. He talked about the honor, passion, and commitment he felt to his decision to serve. He spoke of the challenges and obstacles he encountered upon his return. He talked about the struggles of trying to find his passion and redefine his career after the military. I turned to my husband and said, "I think I can help."

In my career as a corporate and personal brand strategist and counsel for executives of international companies, I have had the honor and pleasure of helping all kinds of people direct their reputation: innovators in education technology; venture capitalists with a passion for sustainability and impact investing; outspoken advocates for the advancement and empowerment of American adolescents; cancer survivors; disabled U.S. war veterans; coaches; consultants; and moms, dads and their college-age kids. My clients aren't celebrities, but they are well known in their respective industries.

My work is primarily with professionals in corporate sectors. My clients tend to be CEOs and executives of leading-edge businesses, and what they all have in common is a consistent passion for the mission of their business and their vision. I am hired to help them define their personal brand, understand their target marketplace, and then create strategies and programs that drive their relevancy into those markets to meet specific business and personal objectives.

What I really get to help these executives do is to create meaning in their work and their lives. My clients recognize the importance of managing their reputations and building authentic relationships though personal branding. The corporate community brings such high competition, that without clearly differentiating each executive's value proposition, the ability to lose purpose is rampant.

I bring experience in the corporate arena to help you understand why and how to position yourself to be competitive in this new world. Military service is vastly different from the service you will encounter on the civilian side, and my hope is that you will gain understanding and insight into your value, your successes, and your need to position yourself correctly to be effective in your new, civilian career.

After that Denver Broncos football game in 2009, I set out to find a group through which I could donate my expertise to help veterans in transition. This was not an easy fete to accomplish! I naively thought every group out there—from the Veterans Administration to independent veterans assistance programs—would want my help. Why shouldn't they? I was a civilian corporate professional offering my talents and skills to help veterans at no cost. Then I learned about military culture and trust. There was a reluctance to engage me and let me volunteer my talents for fear that I was "selling something." In addition, navigating the systems needed to get my help to the actual veterans in transition proved complicated and frustrating.

Through a mutual friend, I was introduced to John Jones, then Executive Director of a group helping veterans based in Philadelphia. John explained that Wall Street Warfighters Foundation (WSWF) was the vision of General Peter Pace, United States Marine Corps (Ret.) and 16th Chairman of the Joint Chiefs of Staff, who created a program to help veterans secure high-paying jobs on Wall Street. The Foundation is helping rebuild the firms on Wall Street by leveraging the talents, integrity, and work ethic of military veterans, and advancing awareness of veterans as valuable employees in Corporate America. In addition, General Pace focused the program on supporting service-disabled veterans, an often over-looked segment of the veteran community.

John was willing to give me an opportunity to bring my program to veterans. The first year I worked with the candidates in the Wall Street Warfighters class was eye opening for me. I brought my traditional personal branding workshop materials and quickly learned how different my program needed to be to serve this audience.

I have worked with Wall Street Warfighters for many years now. I keep in touch with many of the veterans I met through that program—often continuing to coach and advise them as they grow in their civilian careers. Some of their stories are included in this book. Others have helped me edit and refine this book to make sure it serves the intended purpose—to give you the tools, inspiration, and resources needed to transition from a military-to-civilian career. I am eternally grateful to Wall Street Warfighters, John Jones, as well as the current Executive Director, Colonel Katie Haddock, and the entire WSWF Board of Directors for their vision and commitment to keeping veterans informed about the power of personal branding and including me in that effort.

Their work ensures veterans have the skills, training, and insights to become competitive on the civilian side.

Later, I became active with Employer Support of the Guard and Reserve (ESGR), a Department of Defense agency focused on helping employers hire veterans. Through this group, I have learned many of the struggles, obstacles, and passions of employers trying to do the right thing—striving to hire former military—caught in the web of bureaucracy and paperwork to the point of frustration.

In 2012, I became a contributing writer for the careers section of the military website, www.Military.com. Through this site, active and separated military veterans can learn everything from how to secure a home loan to dealing with family stress and finding a civilian job. The stories I hear back from veterans who've enjoyed my articles still surprise me. There is so much frustration, a lack of available tools and resources to help the veteran differentiate themselves, and a sense of disappointment when the veteran tries to bridge the military-to-civilian gap and falls short. My work is to help fix that.

You hold responsibility and accountability for your personal brand. No one can brand you. I will guide you through this process, but you must own the implementation and authenticity needed to be effective. Only then will you experience the true power of personal branding and reputation management.

With gratitude for your commitment, service, and sacrifice,

Lida

About This Book

Business professionals live in the world of differentiation, value propositions, and competitive advantage. Business schools and on-the-job corporate ladder climbing taught us to capture the attention of target audiences with compelling and relevant messaging. At all levels of the civilian work environment, individuals are embracing the power of personal branding to intentionally build a reputation for themselves that attracts opportunities to them.

In this book, I will share my views and approach to personal branding and the processes that will enable you to leverage your expertise and experience in military service to market yourself more intentionally and effectively to hiring managers. You will be armed to now become the person you are meant to be, to attract the clients and relationships you desire, and to draw opportunities to you more easily. Your personal branding journey starts with you and ends with you. It will reflect your experiences, talents, weaknesses, and beliefs. Later in the book, I will share many strategies for you to intentionally put your value into action to bring yourself more joy and wealth and the ability to craft your own legacy.

Veterans Need Personal Branding

I first met Lida Citroen while I was attending financial training with the Wall Street Warfighters.

After a 20-year career in the United States Army, with experience in leadership and fields from infantry to finance and Psychological Operations, personal branding wasn't something I thought about.

What I learned from Lida was amazing: I became aware of how important personal branding is, especially when you are trying to build a positive reputation. Once I learned how to build a reputation, I learned how crucial personal marketing skills are not only for job seeking but for continuing to build a strong background, which could help me build a future customer base or networking contacts. One of the biggest tools that was brought to our group's attention was that we, as individuals, are a complete package. We learned that anything available on social media (and the Internet) reflect on your personal branding. Lida's program shined light on so many things that, before meeting her and taking her class, few of us had any idea about.

Using the tools Lida provided us, I was able to find placement with my company of choice. While working as a Vice President with Drexel Hamilton, I have built a reputation for myself through meetings and accomplishments. With Lida's training, I walked into meetings with a positive image that helped me build a strong customer base.

I strongly recommend personal branding and reputation management training with Lida to any professional who wants to take steps to advance their career.

Jerry Majetich, Staff Sergeant (Ret.), 304th Psychological
Operations Company, United States Army;
Vice President, Drexel Hamilton

As the veteran transitions from military service to a civilian job, I find many of them unarmed with the tools, resources, and insight to compete effectively in finding employment. In all my work with veterans, I see progress forward (veterans successfully learning the skills, techniques, and qualities it takes to compete for civilian work) and the steps backwards (a lack of fundamental understanding of the civilian sector, a lack of resources to help veterans navigate the hiring process). It is surprising that we are not taking more action to address the issue*.

The veteran transitioning from military service is at several competitive disadvantages in trying to secure a job in the civilian sector:

- They are not well networked in their community or industry.

- They have not been versed on social media tools related to employment.

- They are sometimes naive about the corporate nuances and cultural issues that influence hiring decisions.

- They do not know how to translate and explain their service to potential employers.

And the resume is not the answer. I believe personal branding is where we should begin in helping the veteran secure a civilian career. Without a clear picture of the person's values, goals, intention, targets, and vision we cannot possibly help veterans successfully navigate to fulfilling careers outside of the military.

Building your personal brand will require commitment, focus, self-reflection, and self-confidence and will push you to consider your goals and feelings in new ways. I appreciate that I am introducing some new and unfamiliar territory for you, and it may not feel consistent with your service experience and what it took to be successful in a military culture. If you can remember that your civilian counterparts are learning the skills of reputation management and personal branding—and are gaining advantages—you can push yourself to learn these skills as well.

Personal branding may be simple, but it is not easy. It is important to remind yourself that you have been successful before. If you can reflect on the patterns, traits, and attributes in your past successes, you can reveal the strength you will draw on to begin to market your personal brand.

Personal branding begins by understanding what you are passionate about, what you value, and how you live an authentic life.

- What led you to a military career?

- What passions did you bring forward in your service that are relevant as you transition to a civilian career? Similarly, what passions have you subdued, even regrettably, because of military service, expectations, and cultural norms?

- What makes you stand out in the minds of the people you work with?

Personal branding doesn't encourage you to brag, boast, or become arrogant. This is not about making your voice louder. It is about finding a language, message, and position that is understandable and compelling to an audience who needs to find you and hire you. The personal branding process is empowering and gives intention to action that might otherwise feel random.

This book will walk you through the fundamentals of building a compelling personal brand. Through personal branding, you will discover not just WHAT you are but also WHO you are. Ultimately, how do you want to be perceived and remembered? What is your legacy? What will your life mean?

This enables you to decide:

- How you will present yourself

- How you will know who to trust

- Who you will need to know (network with)

- How you will explain your background and skills to get noticed

- With whom you need to build rapport, trust, and credibility

- What you want to be known for

I will then help you understand how to put your personal brand into action:

- How social media can help you promote yourself, build relationships, identify opportunities, and network with influencers who can help you in your career.

- Ways to create the perfect elevator pitch for any situation to let others know what makes you special and unique.

- How to network in a crowded room. Who you need to know. What you need to know about them.

- Tips for studying the needs of your target employer—not just what the job description says.

- How body language and image influence how someone perceives you. Could you be sending the wrong message in your choice of wardrobe or with your eye contact?

- How to align your passions with your work—this is all about creating a roadmap for long-term success. Not just finding a job.

The work I do is strategic, goal-oriented, and feelings-based. We have to understand perception (because it is reality to our audiences). How that hiring manager FEELS about you influences whether they want to give you a chance. I help veterans understand that the words they choose, the people they associate with, and the way they present themselves to others creates a perception about them—they can be in control of how they want to be perceived and drive the opportunities to them.

In my 24 years in the corporate and non-profit business arenas, I've learned a great deal of information and insights to aid you in this transition. Throughout my career, my greatest success has always been in promoting companies, products, or people that come from a place of authenticity and genuineness—realness, in other words.

I also have, like you, a reputation. I created some of that reputation through my actions, with little thought. Other aspects I designed intentionally to ensure that the people who matter to me find me valuable and relevant. That's the part I'm here to share and teach you how to create.

I will share many of the differentiators between a military and civilian career. For instance:

- There are not many "clutch" situations. In the civilian sector, your work will likely not be life or death.

- Pedigrees, certifications, and status are important, but they are not everything. You might feel you are at a competitive disadvantage, but your experience gained in the military experience counts!

- Reputation is very important. How others perceive you, what they believe to be true about you, and how they feel about working with you directly affect the opportunities you will receive.

- Corporate culture and your ability to fit into that culture matter to the hiring manager and supervisors.

- The rules are not always clear or consistently followed. Corporations and many businesses have a loose structure that might feel too fluid for you. You can learn how to navigate this structure. It's important to know you will likely not find the protocol that you had in the military.

While I am writing this for you, the veteran, I recognize that your community and family served along side you. As my colleague, Izzy Abbass, Director of the Boots to Suits Program, University of Colorado Denver, and Staff Sergeant United States Army Reserve, states it, "The whole family serves, but one person happens to wear the uniform. The whole family has shouldered the burden of deployments and military service, and it's important that when we look at the veteran population, we include current and former service members and their families."

"A man who is good enough to shed his blood for the country is good enough to be given a square deal afterwards."

— Theodore Roosevelt

PART I:

Understanding The Transition

Chapter 1:

Approaching the Transition

"The most difficult part of my transition has been applying what I've done in the military to the experience the civilian companies are looking for. I've been supervising administrative/HR offices and have an MBA, but I can't seem to get a foot in the door without specific experience in related fields such as retail, banking, etc..."

— Paul

Each Person's Transition is Unique

I have spoken to and coached hundreds of veterans in the past few years. Never has their transition experience been the same. Some of you went into service taking time out from successful careers. You returned from service to fanfare and job offers—as if you never left.

Others of you had your military careers cut short due to injury—physical, mental, or emotional trauma or disability—forcing your military career to end sooner than you would have liked.

However you came to your transition, now is the time to look forward. We will work together to understand your unique values, beliefs, skills, talents, and dreams. I will help you understand the target audiences in the civilian employment world who might be the best fit for the work you want to do. We will craft your desired legacy, and through that, you will write your brand promise, an articulation of what others can expect in working with you.

We will learn from others, too. While your transition is yours alone, others have had valuable experiences that they generously share in this book. When I suggest networking, you will network with those who can offer unique perspective on your transition because they walked in those same steps. When I discuss finding a target audience, you will include veterans who can advocate and advise you. Learning from others who can guide you and provide resources is very important. Take their advice to heart, and understand what might also make sense for you by listening and learning from their experiences.

Your transition will be a journey. After reading this book, you will have clarity, tools, and ideas to implement, but this doesn't come to life overnight. Understand that transitioning from a culture, work environment, stressful situation, and intense atmosphere, such as what as you encountered in the military, is not easy. You will undoubtedly hit hurdles that will feel insurmountable. You will meet people who seem untrustworthy and disloyal. You will find situations that conflict with your values. This does not mean that the corporate environment is negative.

As you network, learn, develop, and grow your reputation, be sure to take note of others' successes and tips, but remind yourself that your journey is unique to you. No one has the "script" of how this works for everyone. There is no official "way" to find happiness and success in the civilian sector. You will see that structure, protocol, and formality are different in the civilian world. While this might frustrate you at first, you can learn to successfully adapt as many who came before you have done.

Similarly, understand that your transition is your responsibility. You must take accountability for your transition and opportunities you will attract and take advantage of. Many, many people and organizations want to help you and provide tools, but no one can do this for you. As you own your personal brand, so too do you own responsibility for how you behave and execute actions according to your values. If you want people to view you as a leader, you need to act and think like a leader. If you desire a reputation for integrity and honesty, you must behave that way. Branding (as you will learn) is about authenticity and integrity.

As Theresa Z. Blumberg, Colonel, United States Air Force Reserves (Ret.) and Vice President and Co-Founder of Women Veterans of Colorado states it:

> As military members we wear uniforms that tell so much of our story in the glimpse of an eye: our name, rank, branch of service, job in that service, and if we have our ribbons on, one can also read the level and extent of accomplishments, expertise, time in service, combat tours, etc. We become very comfortable in the uniform and the environment that "reads" all about us in a glimpse. Transitioning out of the service and into the civilian world, we must learn to tell the story our uniform once told for us. Just as the uniform did so in a quiescent fashion, so must we learn how to share our vast

experience, training, skills, and expertise in a manner that translates into the needs of the civilian work environment. As we 'doff the blue and don the mufti', we no longer have our story broadcast; rather, we now blend into an environment undistinguished one from another. This is where branding, as Lida Citroen describes it, becomes a critical tool in our job seeking toolbox.

The Jobs Aren't Where You Think They Are

Personal branding is the critical tool that will unlock your value proposition and competitive advantage and will position you to attract the attention from employers.

Most often, unemployed workers turn to job boards, employment exchanges, and online forums. They fill out applications, attach resumes, and craft a somewhat-tailored cover letter and pray for the best.

What's interesting is that according to employers· most job candidates are not sought out on online forums and job boards. In one recent study, 83% of employers said they hire through social networking and personal referral, with only 7% of employees coming through online employment tools.[1]

What does this mean for you? As you consider investing in transition assistance tools, translating your military resume to a civilian one, and

---

[1] U.S. Department of Labor Employment Workshop, Transition from Military to Civilian Workforce Participant Guide, p85

spending hours on the computer filling in forms, consider your personal brand first. Your ability to get recognized, stand apart from other candidates, and clearly define your value to a potential employer is what will get you noticed.

Your Transition is Unique to You

As you navigate this book and your personal brand development, you'll quickly see that for every positive move, there are potential self-limiting moves as well. You will use your personal brand lens and vision to guide you through these opportunities and challenges. When faced with opportunities, contacts, and relationships you will need to use the filter of "is this best for me and where I want to be?" in evaluating them.

You are making the civilian career transition because of your own reasons. Some of you are retiring after a long military career; others of you are separating after injury or other reasons. Some of you are leaving service with college and advanced degrees; while others of you have not advanced your education alongside your military service.

For most of you, retiring from military service is a family decision. You have evaluated your decision to leave the pay certainty and consistency of the military and are entering the civilian world full of expectations and hesitancy of what it will bring. You have likely already discovered that the military and civilian worlds are very different.

Self-Promotion Will Feel Like a Foreign Concept

In speaking with so many veterans and military leaders, I've learned that the culture in which you were taught did not value or support self-promotion. For many of you, this concept (How can I be sure I'm not sounding arrogant, like I'm bragging about how great I am?) will be challenging. I had a Lieutenant Colonel tell me once, "In the face of battle, we aren't fighting for the President of the United States. We're fighting for the person next to us." The sense of connection and loyalty you realized during your military service might feel in contrast to the idea that you now need to learn to promote yourself and your skills. This does not mean you're not supporting your fellow comrades. You are now learning a narrative and language that is needed to compete effectively in the civilian sector. Without the ability to speak clearly and confidently about your skills, values, and passions, you risk being invisible and irrelevant to hiring managers and future employers. I will help you craft that positioning without crossing the line to arrogance and bragging.

When I speak of self-promotion and self-marketing, I am not suggesting you push yourself out front at the expense and to the detriment of those along side you. Rather, you need to learn how to articulate your value to a potential employer to get them to notice you and find you relevant. This is competitive advantage, not cutting others off at the knees to serve yourself. If you sound boring, you will come across as irrelevant. If you can create a narrative about your experience that is unique and compelling, you can highlight your talents and successes without bragging. One recruiter explains it this way: "I had a veteran candidate tell me, 'I just did what I was told...' I looked at her and said, 'Would you read a boring book?' The veteran replied, "No, I would not." I said to her, "Then why would you tell me about yourself in such a boring and uninspiring way?" This recruiter encouraged veteran candidates to practice and rehearse how they explain their successes and accomplishments to get more comfortable with self-promotion.

The reality of civilian-side work is that being able to stand apart from others and being known as valuable and relevant for a specific job/skill/quality is critical to sustainability on the job. Being able to ace the interview is only half the battle. You are trained to know how to adapt and overcome. But on the job you will be required, on a consistent basis, to be able to articulate why you are valuable and relevant and help others see the value in your skills and abilities.

Instead of bragging, become focused and intentional. This book is your first step! The company that will hire you needs you to be clear about your contribution to the project or the team. You are not bragging when you can share your personal brand and value to others in ways that create better alignment, systems, and efficiencies for the group.

Here's how that looks:

Bragging: "I'm so great. Everyone wants me on their team!"

Personal
Branding: "I am passionate about bringing out the best in my team. When I'm leading a team, I call upon my ability to make everyone feel valued and relevant to be a good leader."

Bragging: "I led my teams through more complex scenarios than any business can offer. Hire me and you won't regret it."

Personal
Branding: "Using the leadership skills I gained in my military
              service, I will apply my sharp listening skills, empathy,
              and training to create efficiencies and collaboration
              throughout the organization."

Know, too, that other cultures also struggle with self-marketing and promotion. Years ago, I worked with Aimee (not her real name), an accomplished account executive in the tourism industry. She had been personally responsible for major campaigns and initiatives to attract tourist interest and dollars to areas such as the Middle East and Singapore. Based in Abu Dhabi, Aimee now wanted to pursue similar job opportunities in the U.S. tourism market and realized she had cultural norms to overcome in learning how to market herself effectively in America.

We worked together on her personal branding over Skype and quickly identified several of the issues with which she struggled. Aimee's issues were common to other clients, specifically Asian executives, with whom I've worked. They all had strong cultural connections to navigate when amplifying their personal brand power.

First, Aimee needed to embrace a "self-focusing" approach to positioning herself. She was raised with the understanding that the team/company/community/family is more important than the individual. While this is valid, the premise of personal branding begins with a deep understanding and appreciation for the unique qualities of the individual, not the team, and what that individual has to offer to the team, company, community, and family.

I helped Aimee see that putting her needs and values out front enabled her to understand how she could add value to the organization. This is a good thing! This makes the company and the community better. She learned that focusing first on herself meant she was able to contribute at a higher level.

Next, we looked at how we could package and promote Aimee's unique qualities and skills in a way that differentiated her from her competitors. She was now competing in an American marketplace where terminology, reputation, and skills are very important. We needed to package her international experience in a way that created a unique value proposition and made her stand apart. This kind of "self-promotion" was foreign to Aimee and made her uncomfortable at times.

We spent a lot of time understanding the functional and emotional needs of her American audiences. Through research, interviews, discussion, and surveys, we learned what we needed to do to meld her audience's needs with her abilities and experience and market her brand.

Our targeted and focused strategy meant she would position herself more effectively and proactively, projecting confidence and humility at the same time. Contrary to her previous approach of sending resumes and waiting, we were now going on the offensive and marketing Aimee as a unique asset who was highly sought after.

Aimee is a very authentic, approachable person, and when she saw how her genuineness could still shine through while she aggressively marketed herself, she felt more empowered and in control of her job search process. At the time of this writing, Aimee is considering whether the move to the U.S. is, in fact, her passion. Either way, she is designing a legacy and reputation for herself that is authentic and compelling, in whatever country she decides to call home.

Avoid Becoming a Job Snob

Many veterans today find themselves unemployed and underemployed. They have skills, talents, experience, and expertise—gained in service and after retirement—that should make them highly sought after and desirable by employers. Why, then, do they find themselves working in a job paying a wage below what is competitive or struggling to find work at all?

As you know, when times are tough, the tough get going. That means that regardless of how talented, passionate, experienced, and networked you are, sometimes you have to accept a job that is not up to your expectations or standards. While this can feel like a gut-kick to your ego, it is important to keep your personal brand in perspective. Here are some tips to remember:

- You are not defined by your job. Your job is where you work and how you contribute to your employer, community, and family. If you are working in a job that is not up to your skill set and experience, remind yourself that you might be in a role that is one of survival, not career. You still possess all of your personal brand traits—those might be qualities like integrity, work ethic, commitment to family, passion for helping others, etc. A job that is less than you'd hoped for doesn't change that. It just means you are applying your brand to a position that requires you to be more creative in how you define your narrative (story).

25

If you allow yourself to be defined by your job title, you give your power away. Instead, know that your contribution, reputation, and beliefs are where your value to the company stems from. In times of challenge, employers often "freeze and squeeze" employees to retool and reorganize the skill set. Staying focused on your long-term vision, your passion, and your overall reputation can give you the strength to navigate tough times and act consistent with the legacy you want to design for yourself.

- Remind yourself, you are a veteran! You served your country and many people will appreciate that and recognize your contribution. Others may feel differently or indifferent. You can't change other people. You can, however, continue to hold your head high and remind yourself that you represent the USA brand and all the integrity, honor, passion, and pride it represents.

- Give 100%. Most personal brands are anchored in integrity and doing the right thing. If that is true for you, then regardless of the job, you will dedicate yourself fully and wholly to what is asked of you. Integrity is not discriminating based on a pay scale. If you give 100% of yourself to what you do, you will achieve success and build a reputation as someone with a strong work ethic.

- Work a bigger plan. If you feel you are undervalued and underemployed, then make your current situation part of a greater master plan. Use your time (and income) to set a strategy to move forward. If you are earning minimum wage in a service industry and you used to earn six figures at a desk job, then consider whether you are learning tools and skills that could match up with your past experience to open a new career path. Similarly, if you are only able to secure part-time work right now, consider whether you could supplement your workweek with volunteer work (in a new industry) or even additional schooling and training. This gives you the power to see your current employment situation as temporary and set your sights on a bigger and more rewarding vision.

- Don't forget to dream! Yes, you can actually dream of a career, job, or company that would make you happy. When you dream about "what if...," you create possibility and expand your access to ideas. Imagine what it would be like to have a certain career, dream about a life that involves using certain skills you have, and believe you can be successful. This sets your intention in a powerful and productive direction.

Your personal brand is defined by your reputation. Your behavior and actions reflect your values and build how other people perceive you. That perception is not as job specific as you might think. I've worked with very senior executives who were promoted without warrant and who find themselves struggling with issues of self-doubt, incompetence, and fear of being found out. The job title and pay scale do not determine your self-worth. Only you can do that.

Use Time to Your Advantage

Now that you've picked up this book, you've changed the story of your transition. You have taken the first step to re-write how your career will play out. If you don't continue to take action and move forward, you are missing valuable time and advantage over your competition—civilian and veteran candidates.

A senior hiring manager with a Fortune 500 company and retired Army Colonel told me veterans should use time as their friend. For most military personnel, it is inevitable that one day you will transition to civilian employment in some fashion. Use the time between now and then to learn, plan, and focus on a career after military service that is rewarding and meaningful to you. Build a good network, learn new and relevant skills, build a personal brand, and be ready for the competitive scenarios you will encounter after your military career.

Failure is an Option

I would like to tell you that your transition from a military career to a civilian one will be easy. More so, I wish I could say that because you served your country, you will only experience success in your next job. The reality is, no matter how much planning, preparation, and training you apply to the job search, failure is always a possibility.

My field is personal branding, where I help clients manage and maintain a reputation that meets career and personal objectives. In the face of success, your personal brand reinforces those values that lead to your being able to accomplish goals, meet objectives and succeed. Likewise, in the face of failure, disappointment, and challenge, your personal brand reflects your commitment to the cause, ability to rise above and learn from the failure, and your willingness to try again.

How do you accept failure and keep your composure and reputation intact in the face of stress, frustration, and disappointment?

There is no personal brand strategy for reputation building that doesn't address the inevitable frustrations and setbacks of life. I have one client who claims he is an "expert at failure." He is the president of a very successful technology company and is viewed as an accomplished business leader by many who know him. Yet, he insists that his ability to navigate complex situations, deal with difficult people, and grow a company comes as much from his understanding of stress and failure as it does from what works.

How to Manage Failure

How you perceive failure says a lot about you. Do you see it as a setback or as an opportunity to learn which way doesn't work? Here are four tips to learn about your personal brand and uncover opportunity in the face of setbacks and failure:

1. Assess the situation from all angles. Was there something you could have foreseen if you'd been clearer about your intent? Were you truly overqualified for the job but tried to convince yourself otherwise? Did you have all the data to make a good decision or did you walk into a job interview unprepared or unfamiliar with the company's culture?

2. Take accountability for where you fell short and what you could have done differently. Veterans are often very good at owning their responsibility in a situation, since integrity in the military is

so highly valued. When you can "own" your role, you find it easier to see things clearly, learn from experiences, and move on.

3. Who, in your network, was giving you good advice? Who offered you incorrect guidance? Who gave you emotional support? This will help you know whom you should turn to next time.

4. How much of your decision making and action was emotion based and how much was motivated by logic? Did you over think the situation and neglect your gut feeling? Often times, it is our intuition that guides us in the right direction, and our head gets in the way of doing what we know in our hearts is right.

Success and failure are two sides of the same coin. In every sport scenario, there is a 50/50 chance you will win or lose (unless there is a tie), and that means the odds are usually split. In business, we strive for win-win situations in relationships, transactions, projects, and interactions. When both parties gain, in business, we consider that a successful endeavor.

Remember that your ability to deal with success is as important to your reputation and your career success as your ability to navigate failure.

Pursue Big Company Veteran-Hiring Initiatives

It might feel like a stretch or a dream to work for a big company such as BAE Systems, USAA, Disney, or Microsoft. They are name brands you've grown up with and companies whose values might line up closely with your beliefs. Since they are so large, it's often perceived as impossible to get in the door and actually get a job working there.

Nothing could be further from the truth! I've spoken to hiring managers at many Fortune 500 and Fortune 100 companies who actively seek, recruit, and nurture veteran employees. I'm sure some companies do this for the goodwill and positive public relations benefit, but most of the senior hiring directors I have spoken with have created internal initiatives and systems to make hiring veterans easier. Disney, for example, created a complete website, platform, and set of resources under an initiative called, "Heroes Work Here" to attract veteran employees. They recognize that as a large, well-known brand, veterans are excellent candidates for employment.

Frank, a retired Senior Master Sergeant in the United States Air Force, shared with me his experience working for a large financial institution. Frank had wanted to work for them as long as he could remember—their values and mission aligned with his, and he saw himself working there after his military career. There were no open jobs for someone with his skills when he first approached them. So, instead of walking away, Frank opted to take a 10-month contract (with a cut in pay) to get his foot in the door and establish a reputation in the company. Over those 10 months, Frank built relationships with influencers and supervisors, demonstrated his expertise in problem solving and project management, and learned as much as he could about the business and their clientele. As Frank states it, "I wanted to work with the best of the best. In my mind, this company was it. I just had to get creative about how I would one day get hired."

In another example, Eric, a retired Army Colonel, shared his story with me. He wanted to work for a global Fortune 500 company for as long as he could remember. He learned their product line, memorized their financial history and performance record, and learned all he could about their vision and mission for impact in the world. This was a well-known company who likely had lines of potential employees around the block for every open position, Eric perceived. So he took a unique tact: Instead of calling the human resources department and asking to land a job, Eric called and asked, "Can you help me understand how someone goes about getting a job here?"

This approach proved successful! The answer Eric received was that he should build a network of contacts inside the company and network his way to the top of the candidates for an open position. And that's just what he did. Eric leveraged one introduction into another and then into another one. Because of his deep experience in the military, he was continuously asked to help understand military and veteran issues by these contacts. Soon, Eric became known as the "expert on all things military" and found himself with a lead position in the company,focused on building corporate/military relationships and helping get veterans hired.

James Rodriguez, 1st Sergeant, United States Marine Corps (Ret.); Director, Government Relations, BAE Systems, states it this way, "I speak at career fairs all the time. I see often that veterans are not great at talking about their passions, goals, and expertise outside of military terms. Veterans need to brand their resume for a career path not just a job."

James helps veterans learn how to network by researching companies online, understanding what the industry needs, and tailoring the veteran's experience to those needs and goals of the company. In addition to understanding industry needs, veterans should look deep enough to find the depth of a company's commitment to veteran hiring. As Lieutenant Colonel Chris Ford often states as he interacts with communities around the country, "It's easy for companies to say they are veteran-friendly, it's much harder to be veteran-ready. Companies who are serious about moving away from simple patriotic rhetoric to hire veterans towards a more meaningful commitment to retaining veterans as valuable assets within the company put resources (personnel, programs, affinity groups, mentor programs) behind their initiatives. It is there, where veterans will be more likely to succeed and find fulfillment in their second career."

Seek Out Fellow Veterans

With few exceptions, veterans continue to want to help fellow veterans even after military service. More often than not, I hear stories and examples of veterans coaching and advising new veterans in their transition into the business world. Once on the job, they continue to mentor veterans as they learn more skills and talents and build their career.

John Melia, Corporal, United States Marine Corps.; 1st Lieutenant, United States Army National Guard; founder and former CEO, Wounded Warrior Project, emphasizes that veterans need to continue the bonds developed in military service: "Seek out other veterans in your job search and on the job. The camaraderie you built while active can still offer you support, guidance, and encouragement in your civilian career."

A senior hiring director, and veteran, tells me that he advises veterans to seek out veterans within companies and then network with them! "As a veteran," he notes, "you can call any company and they will want to help you because they want to help veterans." Don't hide or downplay your service commitment. Ask companies about their internal processes and resources for veteran hiring.

Set Realistic Pay Expectations

There is a corporate structure that traditionally rewards expertise, experience, tenure, and value in ways you might be unfamiliar with from the military. In the military, you might achieve an E5 or E6 status, and your pay grade is commensurate with your achievement. When you transfer to the civilian sector, you might realize that your skill level does not come across laterally. Many junior, senior, enlisted, and NCO officers find that their title, status, and civilian pay is not commensurate to their military skill level, pay, and job title. This can be a hard realization.

On the civilian side, pay is also commensurate with experience in the field, so to speak. There is practical and schooled civilian education which corporations and businesses value greatly. Your ability to navigate processes, handle corporate culture scenarios, and build relationships with disparate stakeholders is equally important to your ability to clearly articulate the value you bring to the company. We call this "value selling," and it means that you can tell me the value you will create if the company pays you $X in wages. Just because you earned $50,000 in the Army doesn't mean that's what you're "worth" to an employer on the civilian side.

Chapter 2:

Top 5 Career Myths Dispelled

There are many well-intentioned experts offering advice for career transition and career growth. However, there are also "myths" which many of us encounter that can actually stall or stop your career growth (sometimes before it even begins).

Here are five myths dispelled:

1. **You can do anything you put your mind to.**
   The reality is, we all have limitations—physical, mental, and emotional—which can limit the choices of careers we pursue. As much as I might desire and train to be a professional jockey, at 6'1" tall, I will never be successful at that. Similarly, you might be able to train, practice, and work hard to be a systems engineer for a software company, but if your creative energies tug too hard, you will not be happy. Determination and aptitude are not the only ingredients for career success.

2. **You will have one career in your lifetime.**
   Ask most professionals today and you will quickly realize that

many of them have had multiple careers. I started out pre-law and happened to fall into marketing. I know a web designer who started his career as a professional commercial photographer. He then started teaching himself this "internet thing" and later applied his expertise in lighting, visual design, and composition to be one of the top web designers in his field.

View your career transition as a stepping-stone. You might start with a career in finance, only to find that it leads you to become an author in veteran financial affairs. Or, maybe your next job is in retail, and you build on it to become a consumer marketing professional.

The days of doing one job for the rest of your civilian career are rare. Look at each position as an opportunity to learn something and build your career in total, not segments.

3. **People can't make a living in a bad economy.**
   I once heard it said, "There are folks who can't make a living in a good economy. And, there are people who can make a great living in a bad economy." Don't let the headlines get you down: build your confidence along side your resume and assume you will find a job. There are plenty of people doing fine, despite the unemployment lines.

   Maybe a poor economic climate is a sign that you can find opportunity. Is there high demand for work that you are talented to perform? If the construction industry is down (because the housing market is declining), could you take those skills and work in equipment sales instead? Could you teach a construction class at the local community college? Maybe it's time to look at learning how to do short sales in real estate rather than construction?

4. **You don't have to settle for a job that's not perfect.**
We all have to pay the phone bill and put food on the table for our families. When your vision for the ideal job does not happen soon enough, there are other jobs, which may meet your immediate needs to survive. This is NOT selling out or settling. This is being practical and responsible.

Keep your spirits up and realize you are doing something more noble and practical than starving. You know how to survive. You are a veteran! We all have to make choices, from time to time, that are less than ideal for practical reasons.

When you take that job that is not ideal, ask yourself: What can I learn about myself from this experience (That I am a survivor? That I am a good provider for my family? That I can learn a new skill or talent?)? And do not give up on the career path you have chosen. This unappealing job is just a step in that direction.

5. **Make your goal to send 20 resumes a day.**
As we'll discuss in this book, there are many jobs that are never secured off of a resume. There are resume jobs as well. But it's not the number of resumes sent that equates to career employment. The goal is to focus, target, and customize the resume to see a positive result.

I hear from many veterans who make a goal to send a certain

number of resumes per day in hopes of getting one response. That assumes that all jobs, companies, hiring managers, and recruiters are looking for the same thing. Or, is that candidate actually tailoring each of those 20 resumes every day to meet the specific needs, goals, interests, and culture of that company and recruiter? Doubtful.

Instead of quantity, pay attention to quality. Recruiters are seeing hundreds of resumes for every position (good economy and bad). Make yours stand out and get their interest. This might mean sending less resumes per day, but having a higher likelihood of them meeting their target.

Chapter 3:

Why Hire a Veteran?

As you move into the civilian workforce, it is important to understand the narrative corporations are trying to understand about the reasons to hire veterans. Some companies seek to hire veterans because it reflects a commitment to community and builds goodwill. Others need to meet quotas to secure contracts (often government-related). Still other businesses appreciate the value and values of someone who served and want the talent, expertise, and integrity veterans bring to the workplace.

As Denise Koster, Senior Talent Acquisition Specialist at the Federal Reserve Bank of New York states,

> In my work, I experience amazing moments when the room shifts, attendees engage, and I feel the veterans in my class absorbing information like they are on a sightseeing tour of a new land. In the military, veterans are accustomed to having a plan, receiving intense training, and working together towards a mission (as well as knowing when to adapt and overcome). Their civilian counterparts were busy learning the corporate languages and norms while they were away learning and

experiencing a different set of life skills...they just may not know how to make the translation and use these skills to their advantage. The veterans I meet seem to appreciate a tour guide to help them understand a new culture, learn the language, and learn what is expected of them in the career change/job search. They are exceptional colleagues who understand the value of training, goals and objectives, and teamwork.[2]

In positioning yourself as a veteran, keep certain traits of your brand in mind.

Veterans Are Leaders

Military employees are excellent leaders and outstanding followers. While you have been groomed for a leadership trajectory during your service, you might not want to be a leader in your next career. I remember one Army soldier I worked with who told me, "I'm not seeking to be a front-line leader on the civilian side. Often times, employers think I want to be out front and in charge. I really don't. I've done it, and I'd rather spend my career in a less visible, non-leadership role now." That's perfectly fine! Be sure you communicate that you understand the goals and intensity of the leadership role, and you seek something less high profile in your next position.

Leadership is a mindset, a commitment, and a calling. Jan Rutherford, who spent six years in Special Forces as a medic and "A" team executive officer, spent three years as a military intelligence officer, and who is

---

[2] *Expressing personal views and not necessarily those of the Bank*

currently the CEO of 3t Systems and author of *The Littlest Green Beret - On Self-Reliant Leadership*, tells this powerful story of the mindset of leadership:

> I was fortunate to meet some phenomenal soldier leaders, and I remain an inspired lifelong student of leadership because of their example. On a mountain climb in Colorado in 2010, I realized that the metaphors between climbing and leadership were most applicable if one was engaged in leadership while actually climbing the mountain. On that climb, I met a soldier who had just returned from Afghanistan. In the brief minutes we chatted, we didn't talk about the route, the summit, or the weather. We talked about the team he led in war. Here we were in one of the most beautiful places in North America on a pristine day, and this soldier was talking about people rather than nature. I think I represented someone safe to speak with: I wasn't a fellow soldier, I wasn't his family, I wasn't the press, but he knew I had served.
>
> He told me how he lost eight soldiers as a platoon leader while manning an indefensible base. He cupped his hands and explained how they were placed in a bowl of mountains and expected to defend it from an enemy that had the higher ground. It was heart wrenching. Here was a soldier who just returned from combat, and the first thing he did was climb a mountain. I realized that climbing the mountain for him was a cleansing experience and a place to renew. I later learned the battle he described was the Battle of Kamdesh in 2009, and one of the men from that platoon, Staff Sergeant Ty Carter, received the Medal of Honor from President Obama on August 26, 2013.

Rutherford continues,

> For those of us that climb, the mountain serves as an anvil. The inertia of the mountain allows the energy of climbers to be transferred to their very core. For those who served, they have already been tested, hardened, and developed the necessary skills of a self-reliant leader.

Veterans Are Loyal

Civilians are usually versed in the loyalty and commitment that veterans demonstrate in their dedication to the cause, mission, and to each other. We have seen example after example of veterans risking their lives and safety to protect each other. Many times, veterans are the ones who continue to rise to the occasion to protect fellow citizens. During the media coverage of the Boston Marathon Bombing attack in 2013, we saw military employees and veterans rush in to help the wounded and provide their safety during and after the attack.

Veterans Are Motivated

Military personnel are not encouraged to consider, ponder, or reflect on a mission when orders are given. They act! As such, veterans often bring a unique "can do" attitude and work ethic to their job. They are the first ones at their desk and the last ones to leave. Veterans understand the value of a job well done and strive to meet expectations. This makes veterans great employees and team members.

Veterans Are Professional

Military employees have a high degree of integrity, honor, and work ethic on the job. They also know that appropriate image and appearance are important to creating the right impression. In the civilian sector, employers often hope that the job candidates have been raised to be polite, mindful, creative, and dedicated. The veteran has been taught these traits.

Sometimes, this can show up as a challenge, however. The respect and professionalism instilled in the military results in veterans addressing civilians as "sir" and "madam" uniformly. To a non-military person, this might be surprising and can even be perceived as overly formal. It's important for the veteran to respect the needs of the person he's addressing. If they bristle at that formality of sir and madam, adjust your tone to make the other person more comfortable.

Veterans Are Resilient

Military training instills an ability to make decisions, own personal accountability, and take responsibility for meeting objectives. Veterans have had to navigate and succeeded in diverse work situations and environments, learning the cultural and emotional nuances of very different scenarios. This resiliency makes a veteran an ideal candidate for high-pressure and important work where decision-making skills are valued. Veterans know how to handle stress—on the job and off—and rely on their abilities, experience, and skills to navigate through tough situations.

Veterans Understand Hierarchy

As veterans, particularly if you held a leadership position in the military, you understand that you are part of a larger organization. "We understand that complaints go up ONLY, and once a decision has been made, we know how to delegate it down without bad mouthing higher ups when we don't agree with the decision," says a former Army commander.

There are numerous other attributes, skills, and qualities that make hiring a veteran attractive. Simply Google the phrase, "why hire a veteran," and you will be inundated with information. As Chris Ford reminds me,

> When we talk with employers, we ask them to tell us about the last five employees they fired. Tell us the reasons employees were let go. Without variation, employers fire employees not because they lack some of the skills listed in the vacancy announcement (certifications, licenses, degrees, years of experience); they fire employees due to character flaws such as being disloyal, not a team player, inflexible, and for having little or no buy-in to the organization's mission and goals. We remind employers that veterans are the antithesis of those character flaws. Hire veterans for their characteristics and train to their skills gaps. You'll end up with an amazing talent pool within your company.

As you move through your transition, however, you need to understand what employers are seeing, valuing, and seeking in their teams. If you fit the criteria, leverage your experience and training to make yourself relevant. Talk about your ability to overcome and triumph over adversity. Highlight your training in global recognition and cultural nuances to build trust and confidentiality. Demonstrate to that employer that you have the skills to work on an accelerated learning curve and meet expectations, leading a team or working independently.

Chapter 4:

Corporate Culture 101

The term corporation is used to describe the way a business is organized, managed, and governed. A corporation can be structured in multiple ways and, according to state law, have reporting and tax responsibilities that are unique to the business and regulatory agencies. "Corporate" is used to describe the environment within a corporation or business structured this way.

Corporate leaders and employees do not enter or evolve through the same process you experienced in the military. There is no boot camp or basic training through which all personnel enter and from where individuals perform and ascend through the ranks.

People enter the corporate world at different places, different points, and with different goals and motives. Some people enter the corporate environment straight after college; others go to business or technical school first. For others, the transition to a corporate career comes after a career in a different field, such as a trade or technical environment. We see moms and dads returning to work after raising a family and older people re-entering the corporate world after a brief retirement because of financial hardship. We also see people staying in their career longer because technology allows us to be more mobile and accessible, thus giving us the ability to enjoy a "semi-retirement" lifestyle while still capturing a paycheck.

Because everyone enters the corporate world at a different point and with different objectives, there is no set manual or guidebook for how we will all behave and relate to each other and what we should believe. Every person you will work with has a different background. Similarly, not everyone will look out for you in the way they will look out for themselves. There is a lot of self-focus on the corporate side, rather than the camaraderie you shared in service.

Corporate environments are as unique as the individuals running them. We have the big corporate "giants" who often operate, hire, manage, and drive value in high-profile ways. They are often public companies who are accountable to employees, clients, vendors, and Wall Street investors. We have large privately-owned companies who may have multi-generational family owners. Then there are the small corporate entities, the entrepreneurs, and innovators who fuel the economic engine that is the American Dream.

Some corporate environments are formal and very professional (Wall Street banks, big law firms, and most financial institutions), while others might be more casual and fun (technology companies, creative agencies, advertising, and marketing firms). The culture of the company is also uniquely based on geography. For instance, firms in downtown Manhattan (New York City) tend to be more formal, whereas a California corporation might have a more relaxed environment. Similarly, in Denver we see a lot of Western influence in our corporation cultures.

Often this is because company founders grew up in the area they planted their companies, so that influence is carried through in the work environment.

Culture and "Fit"

Businesses and corporations have a unique culture and hiring managers seek a fit with that culture when they hire. When a job candidate has great skills, experience, and ability but would not work well with the rest of the team or brings an attitude that could prove counter-productive, many recruiters will keep looking. Fit within an organization is paramount to overall business and team success.

A company's culture will reflect how employees feel about working there, their work/life balance, and the style of the environment. Technology companies often have a loose environment where you might find employees wearing shorts to work. Professional services firms, like law firms or financial firms, might require employees to wear a business suit and follow more formal procedures for contacting fellow employees (e.g. sending email requests rather than just stopping by someone's office).

Culture and fit are important for job candidates, too. If you prefer a looser style environment where teams can share a joke and a baseball game together after work, you should inquire about those qualities in an interview. If you prefer a more routine, formal, and structured environment, seek that out. You can learn a lot about a company's culture from their online presence (website, blog, social media posts) and by asking current and past employees.

Some things to consider:

- Do employees operate from a unified and clear company vision, mission, and purpose? Is the company consistent in the values it promotes?

- Does the company support and encourage work/life balance? Do employees take time off when their children need them at home, and is that viewed positively by company leaders?

- Is the environment structured and rigid or more open and casual? If you have a question, are you encouraged to stop by a colleague's office to have a quick chat or would they rather you schedule a meeting in advance?

- Are employees encouraged to spend time together in the community serving others? Is this important to you?

- Are employees motivated by reward or fear? Do people work there because they are growing and contributing or are they afraid they can't work some place else?

- What is the online reputation of the company? Search online review sites and bulletin boards to see how former employees perceive the culture. (NOTE: Keep these reviews in perspective. Often, employees who are fired for poor performance take to social media to vent frustration.)

Gender Issues

I am not a "female" (well, biologically I am but), I am referred to as a "woman" at work. In one of my early veteran workshops, I remember asking the group about a networking situation. In the scenario I painted for them, a woman and a man were standing together. "How would you introduce yourself to the woman?" I asked.

A look of horror appeared on the face of one retired Army Captain in the workshop. "I would NEVER just walk up to a female and try to talk to her, particularly if that could be her man standing next to her."

What?

First, women in the workplace are referred to as "women," not girls or females. Second, in a business scenario, it is perfectly appropriate to introduce yourself to a man or a woman without assuming anything about his or her marital or relationship status. In the scenario I painted, the Captain assumed that there could be something intimate between the two people, and he therefore perceived an interruption as a "come on."

On the civilian side, it would not be uncommon for your supervisor, their supervisor. and the CEO of the company to be a woman. While the ranks of Wall Street firms are slowly embracing women at the highest levels, in 2013, women hold 4.2 percent of Fortune 500 CEO roles and 4.2 percent of Fortune 1000 CEO roles.[3] Anticipate that your job interviewer and their boss could be a woman and a smart one at that!

In the corporate and business environment, gender issues are very relevant. As part of a new-hire orientation in a civilian job, you will likely go through sexual harassment training and will be exposed to protocols and guidelines regarding inappropriate work behavior and conduct.

---

[3] http://en.wikipedia.org/wiki/Women_CEOs_of_the_Fortune_500

In your networking, work relationships, and online behavior, keep your military training in check. Referring to women by terms that are not perceived positively on the civilian side can take away from your credibility or your adaptability to the job.

Pedigrees and Education Count

As the market tightens and the competition for prime job opportunities increases, companies will look at things like education, work experience (especially for premiere companies and in desirable industries), and credentials more seriously. This does not mean that someone without a college degree or with a degree from a non-Ivy league school can't compete. It just means you might have to get a bit more creative.

While it would be great if corporations were more sophisticated in their understanding of formal education versus the benefits of "real life" education (i.e., what you gained in knowledge during your military service), we have to deal with the realities of what formal education brings. In most cases, academic training provides scenarios, case studies and best practices which many corporations rely on to advance their own mission and service. For this reason, a job candidate who brings formal education (particularly from a school such as Harvard or Yale) is presumed to have had access to complex business scenarios and can leverage that knowledge in helping the company grow.

The education hurdle is hard for many veterans to overcome when completing online job applications in particular. The forms companies use to screen and recruit job candidates ask for detailed job and educational experience. There often is not a spot to check, "Instead of going to college after high school, I enlisted and served my country for four years..."

That said, for some veterans, upon return from military service, getting a college or associate's degree makes the most sense to be credible and competitive in their job and industry. This is a decision you will have to make after you understand how to best position yourself for your next career.

Chapter 5:

Trust

I write a lot and am often interviewed by the media on the concept of building, sustaining, and regaining trust. Professionals in all industries, from banking to law to real estate, struggle with the concept of getting others to trust and believe in them.

On a daily basis, each of us is bombarded with seemingly genuine marketing messages—from billboards to online pop-up ads to advertisements posted on the back of restroom stall doors to greetings at networking events—and it feels like we are constantly being marketed trust. What can we possibly believe to be true?

The messages pushed by many companies, as well as independent professionals, is trust: "You can trust me," "I have your back," and "You're in safe hands with me/us."

In developing a personal brand, the focus must be on promoting that which is relevant and compelling to a target audience. While it is true that most target audiences need to trust the company/service/product/

individual who is selling to them, you simply cannot sell trust. Telling someone you can be trusted is not enough.

Here's why: Telling someone you are trustworthy is like saying you're a good kisser—it really is up to others to assign you that quality, not you. Trust is something you develop over time through respect, rapport, and building credibility.

In working with returning military veterans, I've learned that the values around trust and trust building are particularly complex. It took me months of persistence before I was able to get an organization to believe that my intentions and motives for wanting to help veterans with personal branding were genuine and not for commercial purposes. Even as I leveraged my connections in the media to bring a spotlight to the need for more resources—and, yes, I was on camera speaking on the topic of helping veterans—some questioned my motives. Is she using the veteran community for personal gain?

As a veteran, you learned to trust your commanders, your fellow servicemen, and the orders you were given. There is a sanctity and fraternity to military brotherhood (male or female) that is nearly impermeable. This tight-knit bond and unwavering trust serves as a valuable survival skill and creates lifelong bonds that are almost unimaginable to those of us who have not walked in your boots. "During our basic military training (boot camp, basic training, etc.) we learned to trust the soldiers to our left and right," says an Army Sergeant I worked with. "Throughout our service we learned to trust people from various backgrounds and cultural beliefs. We participate in joint exercises with other countries and trust (with limitations) our allied counterparts."

Now, you will need to learn to trust people who do not have military training and ethics and civilians with specific, valuable expertise who want to help you succeed. This will not be easy, I understand.

Trusting others is not the same as being naive. You will not go blindly along with everyone who offers you help or offers you an opportunity. Undoubtedly, you will encounter companies, consultants, and others who want to advise and guide you for a fee, who may not actually have your best interests at heart. Being discriminating and cautious is still important. You still must continue to use a discerning eye and rely on your experience, information, and intuition to make good decisions. But you will need to broaden your acceptance of assistance and guidance from those who have something of value to offer you and from whom you choose to accept offers.

Trust is a Two-Way Street

Enlisting, building, and sustaining trust is tricky. While most people list "trustworthy" as a personal quality on their resume, to be someone who is trusted takes effort, time, and focus.

Trust also needs to go both ways: You need to be trustworthy to others, and you need to be able to trust other people. Undoubtedly there are people in the world who might want to take advantage of you, who do not have your best interest at heart. This is not a civilian/military issue. There are also many, many people who will value you for your contribution, who will recognize your potential, and who will extend resources to help you become who you are meant to be in this world. They will earn your trust if you are open to it.

As you become someone who is trusted in your career, you will build integrity and credibility in the value of your word, and your reputation will reflect this value. As you learn to believe in and trust other people, then you will continue to display humility, vulnerability, and personal accountability as you grow those relationships. Over time, people who matter to you will learn to refer you, appreciate your values, and advocate for your career goals.

In his 2006 best-selling book, *The Speed of Trust*, famed author Stephen M. R. Covey teaches us that: "Extending trust to others rekindles the inner spirit--both theirs and ours. It touches and enlightens the innate propensity we all have to trust, and to be trusted. It brings happiness to relationships, results to work, and confidence to lives. Above all, it produces an extraordinary dividend in every dimension of our lives: the speed of trust."[4]

---

[4] Stephen M. R. Covey, *The Speed of Trust* (New York: Free Press, 2006), 322.

Chapter 6:

Hollywood Misperceptions of the Veteran

As you undoubtedly know, most civilians are not versed in the military way. We do not understand the dedication it took for you to commit your life and your livelihood to military service; we do not know firsthand what combat and fear feel like; and most of us have certainly not lost a friend in war.

What civilians have experienced is often limited to stories in books and movies. Television, movies, and even documentaries attempt to capture stories and tell them in ways that will hold the viewer's attention long enough to make a point or sell advertising. Sometimes, to accomplish this, the stories need to be embellished, and sound effects must be added to make the scene more compelling and memorable.

A retired Marine Corps Staff Sergeant shared with me that in one of his first civilian job interviews, he was asked if he jumped out of helicopters into the jungle and shot up the place, like Charlie Sheen did in the 1986 Vietnam War movie, *Platoon*. (The interviewer asked this question with enthusiasm and excitement, shocking the Sergeant.)

As you transition to work with civilians, keep in mind that for many people you encounter, this is what they imagine when they hear you served in combat, you are a trained sniper, or you were injured due to enemy gunfire or an IED explosion. The civilian sitting in front of you,believes they can relate because they saw Tom Cruise or Bruce Willis in a scene that sounds similar to what you are describing.

This is not a right/wrong scenario. It is what it is. Understanding the depth of awareness of your civilian counterparts is important. When a hiring manager, coworker, or networking contact inquires about your time in service or the nature of your injury or disability, please keep in mind the perspective they have. It is likely limited.

Your job in transitioning is not to fuel the imagination of your civilian counterparts. When you are asked questions by someone you don't know well or if you are unsure how much detail to offer in response to combat- or service-related questions, here are some guidelines to remember (particularly in an interview or networking situation):

- Start off brief. Perhaps just acknowledging where and when you served will quench your audience's curiosity.

- Leave out anything overly graphic, technical, and especially confidential. What you became accustomed to seeing, smelling, hearing, and feeling is still foreign to the civilian and can create images too vivid for your audience.

- Use a transition phrase (a "bridge") to send the question back to the interviewer. You might say, "In combat, I learned how to think quickly, manage stress, respond to changing situations, and motivate others. In this job, are those skills valuable to you?"

Chapter 7:

Civilian Careers Other Than Corporate

As you transition, many of you will seek a new career in the corporate sector—working for a privately owned company or business that is governed by practices that we consider "established and tested." Some of these will be private companies led by a founder and/or family members of the founder or original principals. A public company, by contrast, is overseen by a board of directors and shareholders. They report to a much more high-profile stakeholder, and the pressures and rewards are very different to employees.

You might also consider jobs in the public and government sector. Many veterans find work in government jobs that support and continue the work they did while in service. Or, you might also consider a career in the not-for-profit (nonprofit) sector. These organizations serve a specific community (e.g., children's issues, veterans' causes, disease prevention/research/support, community activism, and so on). Not-for-profit organizations will present as more "mission driven" rather than business or profit driven, as you'll find in a private or public company.

Some of you might seek a career that involves self-employment and entrepreneurship. According to Wikipedia.org, "In political economics, **entrepreneurship** is a process of identifying and starting a business venture, sourcing and organizing the required resources and taking both the risks and rewards associated with the venture."[5] I have heard many professionals remark that the military trains individuals well for a career as an entrepreneur—where your talents and skills of leadership, self-motivation, vision, and consistency with a plan make for a successful venture. If this is your interest, you will be led by a drive to do things your own way and to chart your own course and will be comfortable with the level of risk and instability that often accompanies a new business.

Maybe you'd like to open a restaurant? Write a book? Speak to audiences about a topic you are passionate about? Consult with companies about hiring veterans? Invent a new technology?

A Syracuse University Institute for Veterans and Military Families study reported numerous advantages that veterans bring to the entrepreneur role. The study notes that high-performing entrepreneurs and innovators tend to be successful in managing risk, identifying reward, and navigating the complexities of entrepreneurship because they possess a strong need for achievement and can make decisions in the face of high stress, dynamic environments. Successful entrepreneurs are comfortable with independence and autonomy as well. The study points out that military service instills in veterans characteristics consistent with

---

[5] http://en.wikipedia.org/wiki/Entrepreneur

successful entrepreneurs: high need for achievement, trust, strong comfort with autonomy and dynamic decision-making processes.[6]

"According to multiple studies by the U.S. Small Business Administration and others, military veterans are twice more likely than non-veterans to pursue business ownership after leaving service, and the five-year success rate of ventures owned by veterans is higher than the national average."[7]

Other Career Options

There are many options for civilian jobs after service. Some jobs require the use of a uniform, script, and approved working tools (e.g., a mechanic, waitress, plumber), and some allow you to have more flexibility. Some jobs require additional training and certification (e.g., teacher, lawyer, accountant, stockbroker), and some jobs require much less.

Whatever direction you move toward in your next career chapter, consider the environments where you are most comfortable and the types of people with whom you do your best work. Consider jobs in blue collar sectors (trade jobs) and white collar industries (corporate, professional), and self-employment (entrepreneurship).

---

[6] Syracuse University Institute for Veterans and Military Families, "The Business Case for Hiring A Veteran. Beyond the Cliches," Syracuse University Institute for Veterans and Military Families Website, http://vets.syr.edu/wp-content/uploads/2012/08/The-Business-Case-for-Hiring-a-Veteran-3-6-124.pdf, (accessed January 2, 2014).

[7] Ibid.

In addition to security and government jobs (where a lot of veterans start), consider careers in fields such as:

- Construction
- Real estate (sales, management)
- Property management
- Marketing
- Sales (product, service)
- Management
- Project management
- Product development
- Retail (sales, management)
- Writing (authorship, journalism)
- Internet/mobile technology
- Web design
- Social media management, design, implementation
- Coaching and training
- Graphic design, art
- Printing, production
- Consulting (business, procurement)
- Manufacturing
- Financial services (accounting, investment, brokerage)
- Environmental (studies, finance, science)
- Oil and gas (field work, transportation, production, sales, management)
- Teaching
- Veteran services
- Medical (physical therapy, doctoring, counseling)
- Sports (management, coaching, training, development, sales)
- and many others!

"To Thine Own Self Be True."
- William Shakespeare

PART II:

Getting Started:
Your Personal Brand

Chapter 8:

What is Personal Branding?

The term personal branding can mean many things. Some people call personal branding the technique you use to self-market and present yourself (how you dress, speak, and act). Others say it's what public relations professionals do for celebrities to make them marketable as spokespeople. Still others refer to interviewing skills, resume writing, and even portrait photography as personal branding.

Personal branding is not just about designing "packaging" for yourself or about selling yourself as something you are not. Your personal brand is your reputation, your values, and your purpose all wrapped up into one neat promise. Your brand identifies what makes you unique and clearly communicates that uniqueness to an audience that needs you.

Your brand represents your personal values, beliefs, and "moral compass." It might also represent how those values come to life in your interactions with others. Developing your personal brand gives meaning to something intangible. It characterizes the qualities people might feel when they work or interact with you. Others may view you as "easy to work with" or "non-collaborative" or "pushy." These are all impressions they may have about you, based on what they have experienced.

Branding is all about feelings and emotions. Unlike marketing, which is when we direct an audience to action (interview me or hire me), branding sets the emotional expectations and promises between you and your target audience. Sometimes it is that thing that people can't quite put a finger on, but it guides them to want to involve you in a great project, refer you for an excellent position or promote you to a better job. You just make them "feel" like they want you around.

Everyone has a personal brand because we're all known for something. You may not be known for what you want to be known for, but you are known for something. Your reputation may have been the guiding force behind most of your success to date, or it may have been what has been holding you back from achieving your dreams.

Ultimately, your brand is your legacy. It is the way you are known today and how you will be remembered when you leave this earth. Your legacy is the most real representation of how you lived, behaved, and interacted with others and how they felt about you. Instead of leaving that to chance, personal branding puts you in the driver's seat—you control and direct how others see you, feel about you, and the value they assign you!

Chapter 9:

Why Do Veterans Need a Personal Brand?

Judgment and perception are part of our lives as humans. We instinctively judge other people—it's our nature. We form opinions about people based on how they act, what they look like, how the sound and how we feel about them. And that judgment is important as a survival skill—on the battlefield and in business.

According to the Merriam-Webster Dictionary, judgment is, "the process of forming an opinion or evaluation by discerning and comparing; an opinion or estimate so formed."[8]

As you undoubtedly experienced in your military training, being able to "size up" the enemy or a potential opponent is critical to your survival, the protection of your fellow troops, and the success of your mission. Whether you serve at 30,000 feet or on the ground, in military service you learned to form opinions that would advance your situation and position strategically. In a civilian work environment, you will also need

---

[8] http://www.merriam-webster.com/dictionary/judgment

to judge things like whether your colleagues can keep information confidential, if you can rely on them to meet goals and expectations, and whether you want to bring them on an important sales call. Judgment is the instinctual "gut feeling" we have about others, right or wrong, and our experiences create the filters we use to evaluate.

In forming judgments about people, we look for what we believe to be "normal" for that person. (This is particularly true in studying body language, which we will discuss a bit later on.) Is that person normally grouchy and pushy? Is she usually cheerful and upbeat? "Norming" is what enables us to relate to each other in ways that feel safe and predictable. No one can be perfect all the time—we all have bad days. When I see someone who I know to normally be generous, happy, and approachable, screaming at a checkout clerk in the grocery store, I don't suddenly perceive him to be arrogant, bullish, and loud. Instead, I write his behavior off as him "having a bad day." On the other hand, if I begin to see that behavior repeat itself, I question my belief about that person and begin to see the new behavior as normal, causing me to see him in a completely different light.

The fact that we judge other people is not a bad thing. As I stated, there are human instinctual reasons for it. But you want to make sure that you are being judged for your true value and in a way that reflects who you truly are, rather than leave it up to chance. This is what personal branding is all about: ensuring that others see you in a way that is consistent with your values, beliefs, and the perception you want to create.

There are many reasons people look to personal branding. As you transition from a career in the military field to a civilian environment, there will be many new situations you will find yourself in. Having a set of guidelines and filters (your personal brand) will remove a lot of the guesswork. When you've built your personal brand, you won't stress about what to wear to an important interview, what font your resume is typed in, or how you answer the question, "What is important to you?" You will have tools to respond to situations you haven't been in and resources to draw upon for situations that prove familiar (even if they are still challenging).

When you take the time to define and build the reputation you desire and create your personal brand, your target audience will know who you are, what you do best, and why they need you. As we talk about translating your military experience, successes, and accomplishments into civilian-speak, your personal brand vision will be at the core. The best language and messaging in the world can't paint as wonderful a picture of your value and worth to an employer as your brand can!

Personal branding will help you no matter where you are in life: just graduating from college and starting your career, transitioning from service to civilian, or entering the retirement phase of your professional life. Who you are and how you represent yourself is the focus of a legacy that has meaning, purpose, and intention.

Here are some additional reasons to develop a personal brand:

- **You'll live more authentically.** Often times, when veterans strip away the uniform and the title, they feel amiss with how they can express their sincerity and genuineness to others. There is no "shield" explaining who they are, and therefore they must find a way to connect that comes from the heart, rather than rank.

Personal branding is about owning your own voice and feeling empowered in the uniqueness you bring to the world. For this reason, we always start with authenticity. Authenticity is what makes you, you. It is the genuine you that sometimes hides because you are unsure, unaware, or have been trained (conditioned) to assimilate and blend in. You are not like anyone else. Only you possess the combination of values, skills, beliefs, and experiences that make you the individual you are. When you can recognize your values (strengths and weaknesses) and project yourself authentically to others, they begin to see you for who you truly are and appreciate the value you contribute to the experience. In turn, you'll find it takes less effort to decide how, where, and when to engage with others because you'll consistently come from a place of sincerity.

In 2009, my new client, Cathy, called me from Boston. She had a problem. She was to give her approval on a new website for her consulting business, and something just didn't feel right. She couldn't put her finger on it, but something about the new website didn't sit well with her.

Together, we decided that a personal branding project was in order. Cathy's business leveraged her reputation and her personal credibility. It was a direct extension of her personality, reputation, and network of contacts. Therefore, it needed to match up closely with her personal brand. Knowing this, I chose not to look at the website design until after we had done our work together.

Through this work, I learned that Cathy was passionate about action. She talked fast, ran ideas together quickly, and was attracted to clients who were very Type A—energetic and results-driven. Cathy was upbeat, happy, and creative. A successful sales executive for many years, she had an extensive network of high-performing clients and prospects.

After assessing the results from her brand feedback and dissecting the functional and emotional needs of her audiences, we learned that her target audiences truly appreciated the fact that she moved fast, produced results, and delivered a high degree of transparency to her process.

Then I looked at the website mockup. No wonder Cathy's stomach hurt! Her website designer had chosen subdued colors, passive imagery, and header copy that read, "Are you tired and burned out? We can help." How uninspiring and demotivating!

In her brand framework documents, I had provided Cathy with new language, marketing direction, and tone suggestions. We shared this framework with her web designer, and although Cathy couldn't figure out why the website didn't feel right to her, within a couple of weeks the designer came back with a home run! The new site reflected her energy and attracted the attention of her dynamic target audience; the copy was bold and direct, just like Cathy. She told me months later that her website became a true reflection of who she wanted clients to get to know. The mistake she'd made, as she described it, was focusing on "decorating" before building the "foundation."

- **You'll be distinguished from the competition.** Setting yourself apart from others who might offer similar value allows you to avoid what I call the "commodity sale," where your audience chooses based on price (wage) alone. Here's an example: If you go to the grocery store looking for laundry detergent and you don't care about a specific brand—if the brands don't mean different and compelling things to you; if you consider all laundry detergent to be created equal and expect they will all deliver the same result—how do you choose? Most often, you will buy the cheapest one. After all, why would you pay one penny more for something you consider to be the same?

If you are not seen as unique, compelling and relevant to your employer or potential employer, then you leave to chance the possibility that she might choose someone else for a promotion or new job based only on who's the cheapest to hire. Or, the employer might perceive all veterans to be the same. If your employer simply looks at skills, time on the job, certifications and credentials but does not see your unique value and brand assets, she might choose your competitor because they command a lower salary. That's not how anyone wants to compete! We don't want to be chosen because we're the least expensive solution among a lineup of options. As a veteran, you need to use the personal branding skills and attributes that set you apart to differentiate yourself from civilians and veterans who are competing for the same opportunities.

Whether you are applying to college, graduate school, or a job, your ability to clarify your value, make yourself relevant, and help your audience see you as compelling is critical to gaining the opportunities you desire.

- **You will become known for something.** When you sell something, you must have a firm grasp on what separates it from the others. What is the unique selling proposition? The same goes for people. If you have a strong personal brand, your audience begins to see you as a visionary, leader, or collaborator, and you become more valuable. You become visible for qualities you have intentionally designed and put forth through your actions and are no longer just another faceless commodity among many.

- **You'll create an emotional connection with your target audience.** On paper you might look fantastic, but how I feel about you as a person will lead me to hire, promote, or buy from you. On the other end of every purchase is a person, a human being. As humans, we act on emotion. Remember the last time you bought something you didn't need? Often, we purchase something because the emotional side of our brain gets wrapped up in soaking in the experience. Retailers count on this! They create emotional experiences in their stores—from the edgy, clean, creative feel of an Apple store to the sexy, expensive, exclusive ambience of a BMW showroom—and we're drawn in. We engage and spend when we feel that emotional connection.

  Branding is about emotions. It sets the expectation for the emotional benefit our audience will gain from working or being with us.

- **You'll become more focused, more intentional, and more values-based in your search.** A strong and powerful personal brand lives through how you intentionally promote its value at every touch point—from the ways you interact and engage with others in person (including the words you choose and the way you dress) to the way you present yourself online in social media. Before you can project a brand, you first must think about who you are: your goals, your desired reputation, your successes, and your challenges. Once you determine these, making decisions on a daily basis becomes infinitely easier, faster, and more rewarding.

Being focused and intentional means you can use your values and brand to help you align with companies, partners, colleagues, and teams that support your vision and legacy, instead of detract from it. As Kevin Preston, Director of Veterans Initiatives at The Walt Disney Company shared with me, "My path here was not novel. I simply used what the military taught me and turned it inward; I became focused and strategic, and I used time as my friend, not enemy." Kevin shares his experience on the company's blog:

> I started my search when I was still seven years out from retiring. As a mid-level officer, you know you have an expiration date on service—I wanted to be in control of my future, not be surprised one day when I had to create a new career for myself.
>
> As long as I could remember, I'd admired Disney—I valued what they stood for as a company, the communities they'd built and the brand they'd stood by through many generations of leadership. The Disney values aligned well with my own. While still in the military, I decided I wanted to work for the company, but I didn't know how to get a job there. I found a colleague who had been through the Disney Internship Program. I got a name and contacted Disney's HR department, not to ask for a job but to learn about how to get a job. I started

to talk to people who worked there and then talked to more people who worked there. In almost every discussion, they had questions about the military and I had answers. I became a resource, advocate and counsel for military insights at Disney. I started to build my brand.

Over the course of next several years, my Disney network grew. I continued to learn about the culture while answering their questions about the military. I became seen as someone who was knowledgeable and approachable and as someone with the relevant insights and answers for hiring veterans. I pursued a Masters in Business Administration to compliment my Masters in Education and I built my resume, all to establish a brand for myself so I'd be ready to find a job after leaving the military. That's when my current role emerged – something I'm thankful for every day.

I advise veterans to pursue a "values-based job search" and identify the companies that align with their beliefs and goals. Then start networking your way in! The military taught us values, that doesn't leave you after you retired or separate.[9]

- **Your target audience will become more evident.** When you build a personal brand, the process requires you to look at the audiences who need to find you compelling and relevant. This focuses your efforts from "anyone who could possibly buy from me" to a targeted group of individuals who understand and want what you have to offer. The foundation for personal branding is based on the

---

[9] https://thewaltdisneycompany.com/blog/inside-look-heroes-work-here-disneys-director-veteran-initiative

Laws of Attraction—what you focus on, you will attract. Theories on the laws of attraction (in the realms of physical science, sociology, and psychology) date back to the early 20th century. The basic premise is that if you think positively and with intention, you can manifest greater opportunity than if you dwell in the negative or neglect to think with intention. By taking control and ownership of your personal brand—your reputation, destiny, and legacy—you can begin to attract the people and opportunities that align with your vision. If you neglect your personal brand, you leave to random "luck" what you might attract, positive or negative. If done well, your return on investment (ROI) increases, and your effort decreases.

- **You'll build credibility.** A personal brand allows you to build credibility because the more you're known for something and the more you fulfill that expectation, the more you build integrity around the promises you make. If you are valued and trusted—if you've established credibility—people want to be around you and do business with you. Being trusted by clients, peers, and colleagues is critical and is achieved by paying attention to your personal branding and delivering on the promise of that brand at all times.

- **You'll make it easy for others to offer you opportunities.** When your personal brand is clearly defined, intentionally marketed, and targeted to a specific audience, your audience knows just what you stand for and can easily understand how you might help them. Likewise, your audience learns how they can help you.

Chapter 10:

Important Elements to Build Your Personal Brand

Your personal brand must be CLEAR to be understandable

There are four Cs and an A to remember when building a successful personal brand. First, your brand needs to be clear. It's up to you to clearly articulate to others what makes you unique. If you don't clearly communicate your value, you could fall victim to the "commodity sale" (discussed in Chapter 10), where you look like every other job applicant. Let's say that I'm considering two aviation specialists to work in my company, and you are one of them. In addition to technical training, I'm seeking someone for this job who is easy to get along with and who will fit in well with the team.

Both of you (candidates) have similar skills and training, bring the right credentials, and have the same number of years of experience. But you are known by others as being easy to get along with, proactive (thinking ahead), and as someone who will go above and beyond what's needed to get the job done. You also make me feel like you appreciate my personality and are loyal and committed to your work (you're a veteran, after all). You and I seem to laugh at the same jokes and understand the same sense of urgency for the business. In my mind, you're not measured side by side with that other aviation guy. You have value and uniqueness: you are differentiated and somebody I want to work with. I will even pay a little bit more for the opportunity to work with you.

In a 2012 Entrepreneur Magazine article, the author notes, "today's most trustworthy brands have created relationships with consumers through experiences that trigger a visceral response."[10] That response causes us to believe we know and trust what that brand is promising. It's why many women walk into the laundry detergent aisle at the grocery store and buy Tide. "Tide makes me feel like I'm a good mom." "It makes me feel like I can take care of my family, and I know my clothes will come out clean." "Tide is special, and my family deserves it."

At every step, we want to use words and marketing strategies that reflect our differentiation. What is your brand and how are you special? What are you passionate about? What makes you different from the person sitting next to you? You could be sitting next to someone with the same skill set, almost identical education and training, the same hair color, and even the same set of contacts. What makes you different? You must clearly communicate, through everything you do, why you are the ideal choice, and make yourself relevant to that target audience.

---

[10] Andruss, Paula. "Secrets of the 10 Most-Trusted Brands,". Entrepreneur. http://www.entrepreneur.com/article/223125#ixzz2nNxTtrej. (accessed January 2, 2014).

Create a COMPELLING Brand to Get Noticed

Second, your personal brand must be compelling. Why should your target audience care about you? You (and your mother) might think you are the greatest asset any company could hope to employ, but personal branding is not all about you. It's also about the needs, interests, and goals of the audience you are targeting, too. You need to make sure the message you deliver to that audience is compelling and clearly articulates why they should care. Think about my example of the two aviation specialists. The one I find compelling is the one who ensures that I recognize the unique skills and traits he brings to the engagement. He makes sure that I see his value and his personality and that I feel reassured as I ask questions during the interview. He makes sure I find him compelling.

As an Air Force Lieutenant Colonel I work with tells it:

> When I worked as the Chief of Protocol, I had to interview Airmen that the Command Chief had selected to serve as one of my assistants for a year period. There were three candidates that made the final records cut. Now, bringing an Airman into a serious environment such as the Office of Protocol is risky business….but we needed the help….we (me and my one civilian employees) were drowning in work. All three of the Airmen were sharp; all had been screened by the Command Chief, but since it was my shop, I was given the ultimate decision. One of the candidates, I could eliminate immediately (in the first two minutes of the interview). His attitude wreaked of someone who'd rather be anywhere else, and who could blame him? Protocol is a tough business. It eats its young. It is a high-profile job that requires exhausting attention

to detail to do it correctly. I didn't need an Airman with an attitude; I had to answer to my Vice Commander for things I couldn't control.

I narrowed the choice down to two candidates; everything about them was the same as far as attitude, appearance, and records. The distinguishing mark for me was that the one I ultimately selected was a passionate person with a lot of energy in the interview process. Also, before the interviews I would take one of the pictures hanging on my office wall and tilt it to a slant. The last candidate may have noticed, but I couldn't be sure. The candidate I ended up selecting was slightly distracted while talking to me, I caught her looking at it a couple of times and asked her what was wrong. She told me that the crooked picture on my wall was bothering her. That was the clincher for me! She was hired because her brand sold me. She was compelling.

CREDIBILITY is at the Heart of a Powerful Personal Brand

Then, you need to demonstrate that you are credible. Credibility and integrity are not traits you can promote just by saying, "My personal brand is about trust!" Credibility and integrity are intangible; they are experienced, proven, tested, and consistent. They are the values your "fans" will refer to as they sing your praises, refer you to prospects, and nominate you for recognition. Credibility means others will vouch for you, endorse you, and recommend and refer you. This is critical in a job search when you might lack the experience or expertise to be positioned competitively. Having others promote you will be very helpful. For this to happen, however, they need to see you as credible.

Your Personal Brand will not Succeed if it's not CONSISTENT

The only formula I know for building credibility within a personal brand is a pretty simple one. It starts with articulating your values: telling people what you stand for, what matters to you, and what you will fight for. And it ends with being consistent (the fourth C) with the values and beliefs you advocate. By doing so, you build a reputation of integrity. My new graphic designer will ensure that when I see her website, talk to her former clients, read her blog, and begin working with her, the traits and values she conveyed in our first meeting are consistent across all her other points of marketing herself.

Here's an example: Let's say you are passionate about honesty and integrity. You believe people should see you for who you are. "What you see (with me) is what you get," you often say. It is vitally important to you that people learn to trust that you are a man of your word, that there are no "smoke and mirrors," and that you are what you say. So, what happens if a recruiter goes to your online profile and sees you representing yourself differently? Maybe they see you repeatedly speaking ill of another colleague or competitor in a military-to-civilian transition group on LinkedIn. Is that the behavior of someone who is honest and transparent? I don't think so.

People need to know that if your values involve qualities such as being approachable, warm, and inviting, then they should be able to walk into your office if they need something, and you're not going to shut the door in their face. They need to know that if they leave you a message, you're going to call them back. If they have an issue they need to talk to you about, you'll make time for them. Consistency is critical in building your personal brand. Otherwise, others will see your values as just lip service, spin or fluff. When we talk about credibility and integrity, we're talking about acting according to your values. It's the walk-the-talk proof of what you hold out to be true. Through repetitive consistency, others will believe what you tell them and show them to be true. This is how you build trust.

AUTHENTICITY is at the Heart of Any Personal Brand

I define authenticity as "living the core goals, beliefs, and values that guide your emotional, spiritual, and intellectual self and that present through behavior." In other words, when you are your most genuine self, you are being authentic.

The work I do is all rooted in authenticity, that deep-down truism about you as a person that makes you unlike anyone else. It is your genuine spirit, the you that is the most real. To be in touch with your authenticity means you see yourself as a whole—the good and the bad, the successes and the failures—and you own it all. You have humility in knowing what your limitations are and where your passions stem from. To be living an authentic personal brand is to be the most empowered person you can possibly be. To be authentic is to live a life where you (the real you) are always present. Authenticity is at the truest core of what we do in marketing our value to others.

When we encounter you, are you being authentic? Are you representing yourself as you or as someone you think we'll like? Being authentic means that across situations, I will experience you—and your commitment to your values—consistently.

Since a brand is a promise of an experience, an authentic brand is one that has a consistent, dependable experience attached. Each time I experience you, I know I can expect you to be yourself (e.g., qualities such as friendly, honest, collaborative, inquisitive, etc.). I don't have to worry that you will try to be someone you're not just to impress me.

Example of Authenticity:

I worked with a former TOPGUN pilot who'd spent the recent 20 years as an entrepreneur and innovator in the energy sector. Don had been instrumental in designing, negotiating, and directing large teams and was lauded for his skills of financial acumen, innovation, teamwork, shareholder management, and board management.

When I worked with Don (not his real name), he was carefully scripted. He had spent years being coached by PR teams and executive coaches, all giving him well-crafted key messages. His presentation skills had been honed over many years of public exposure.

At the time I worked with Don, he was transitioning out of his role as CEO of a start-up energy company, poised for success and growth. This presented a unique time in his life: No longer would his messages be prepared for him. He was on his own now.

Our work together revealed many "ah ha's" as well as confirmed some beliefs. Don was great at building teams. He loved to mentor young people who were passionate about the energy industry. He reflected back (often) on his career as a TOPGUN pilot—what it meant to have others trust him with their lives and how it felt to go "off radar" and rely on training and instinct. His military experience was part of his passion, his DNA, and his motivation. He believed passionately in transparency and honesty. All of these authentic passions, character traits, and beliefs gave Don and I a platform from which to design his personal brand strategy and create the next chapter in his personal and professional life. We designed a personal brand strategy and tactical plan that Don found easy to implement because it was based on his authenticity. For once, Don could go off the script and be himself, and that was exciting to him!

"Your time is limited, so don't waste it living someone else's life. Don't be trapped by dogma—which is living with the results of other people's thinking. Don't let the noise of others' opinions drown out your inner voice. And, most important, have the courage to follow your heart and intuition."
-- Steve Jobs,
Apple Co-Founder and CEO

PART III:

Building Your Personal Brand

Chapter 11:

What is Your Current Brand?

You already have a personal brand. Through your work and service, you've built a reputation in the minds of other people. Think about your current brand. What drives you? What sets you apart from the person sitting next to you? What makes you special? This level of introspection, of self-reflection, is not easy for most people since personal branding is often counterintuitive to how we were raised. Particularly coming from a military experience, where team and group are emphasized over individual, spending the time and energy to examine your reputation, goals, vision, and passions might seem challenging.

A popular Japanese proverb states it this way: "The nail that sticks up gets hammered down." In the military, your experience and training taught you that to avoid ridicule and targeting, and to get through tough situations, conformity was often the best option. Questioning authority, challenging the norm, and standing apart often got you punished. As your supervisors were building you into a military leader, it was important (if not crucial!) that you focus on platoon/squadron/team before yourself. You didn't brag, promote, or market yourself. You were taught to take "I" out of your vocabulary.

As children, we were told to blend in, not to make waves, and not to call attention to ourselves. We were told just to fit in with the others. This is especially true for women. Magazines, TV shows, how-to books, and gurus constantly encourage us to look and act like everyone else who is "successful" or "accomplished." We're not taught to think about what makes us special and unique. We're not taught to self-promote and boast.

In the civilian marketplace, it's essential to be able to articulate what you offer the world and how that is unique from what others are saying. You need to take ownership and accountability for projecting and demonstrating value if you expect to get the benefits of a powerful reputation.

Example:

James Rodriguez, 1st Sgt., United States Marine Corps (Ret.), shared with me how his reputation and brand helped him to get noticed and stand apart from others when the prime opportunity presented itself:

> I spent 21 years in the Marine Corps before my transition to a civilian career. During my last year in service, between 2008 and 2009, I was stationed with Wounded Warrior Battalion West, located at Marine Corps Base Camp Pendleton, California, to assist in the command's early stages of development. As part of the battalion effort, I was assigned as the detachment First Sgt. at Naval Medical Center San Diego, where I led the development of the

Marine detachment and along with the staff assisted in building it into a great place for Wounded Warrior care and recovery. Within the final phase of recovery, the staff and I helped wounded Marines and Sailors understand how to navigate between employment opportunities and higher education resources as they transitioned out of military service.

During one of our senior level staff meetings with the Admiral, who was in charge of Naval Medical Center San Diego, I was provided with a job announcement for a company that wanted to start a new program, focused on employing wounded veterans. Based on my work within the detachment, the Admiral understood that I was passionate about helping my fellow Marines and veterans in general and that I possessed the skills and drive to build a program like this; therefore, she recommend me for the position.

In 2009, I was hired by BAE Systems, a global defense, aerospace, and security company, employing around 88,200 people worldwide. My job was to create a program which would assist in the placement of wounded veterans from the Iraq and Afghanistan wars in positions across the business that were ideal for transition from the military into the corporate world. In my first year, our goal was to get one Wounded Warrior hired; we hired 16.

By 2013, we had hired more than 140 Wounded Warriors and a few hundred veterans at more than 38 locations across the United States.

If I was to reflect on why the Admiral would recommend me for this great opportunity, I believe it was because she understood my values and talents. I had been building my personal brand with her, without really knowing it. She saw me as someone who would go above and beyond to help, who had a cross cultural mindset for collaboration and problem solving, and who had excellent coordination and program management skills. I had also been clear with her (and others) about my goals and desires to bring the military perspective into the corporate arena. This made it easy for her to recommend me for the BAE opportunity.

Take Inventory

Personal branding starts with you and your authentic values, beliefs, and goals. Begin thinking about what motivates you. You might say, "I enjoy being around people," "I love the thrill of the chase;" "I'm passionate about figuring out problems and bringing solutions no one else could see;" or "I've received a lot of feedback that says I'm a really good listener." Those might be the qualities you begin with to understand your current brand. Consider your response to these prompts:

- Who inspires me (military authors, my colleagues, parents, commanders)?
- What skills am I known for (leadership, problem solving, resiliency, team building)?
- What skills am I good at but do not enjoy (math and analysis, collaboration, management)?
- What skills, talents, or credentials do I feel I'm missing (college degree, MBA)?
- What motivates me? For instance, am I driven by the need for respect, acceptance?

Next, consider five key words that describe you. Think beyond the obvious ones—ethical, trustworthy, and hard working—because most of your competitors (military and civilian) are saying those same things. Dig deep to understand what key words describe you and set you apart. This is certainly an exercise you can come back to but getting those five current brand words is very important.

You might find that some of these key words fit you:

- **Resilient** (I can focus on a task and find the resources needed to accomplish a goal).

- **Tenacious** (I won't stop until the mission/project is completed. My goal is to exceed expectations and deliver more value than my employer expects).

- **Faithful** (I do my best work when I can believe strongly in the values of the company and the people I work with. My own faith and values anchor me in a strong work ethic).

- **Humorous** (I like to make people laugh and feel good. Life is stressful; I want to be the person who adds humor and joy to the workplace. My squadron-mates could always count on me to add levity to tense and stressful situations).

- **Specialist** (I can confidently hold myself out as an expert and specialist in my field. I bring a level of training and real world expertise that is unmatched in the business environment).

- **Passionate** (I see IT solutions as a direct reflection of a company's vision. For me, passion and problem solving go hand-in-hand. I am passionate about creating solutions that serve my employer's mission and purpose).

- **Attentive** (I pay attention to the small details, the nuances that others overlook. Sometimes those nuances can make or break a project).

My five current brand keywords are:

1. _____

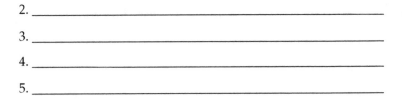

2. _____

3. _____

4. _____

5. _____

Authenticity Isn't Easy

To uncover your authentic self, here are some tips:

- **Reflect on your passions.** What do you enjoy doing? What do you love to talk about? What makes your heart race with excitement as you reflect on it?

- **When do you feel "inauthentic"?** When do you find yourself not acting like yourself, going through the motions, trying to be someone else? Is there a pattern to this behavior?

- **Who do you enjoy being with?** Adults? Children? Creative types or more analytical people? When do you feel most "like you"?

- **What feedback is most positive?** When you reflect on feedback you've received, what makes you happiest? Is it a comment like, "You're always on time"? Or, "You have such respect for our company protocol—showing up on time shows us you care about the company?" Look for other examples of times you have shared this same behavior—did you get similarly positive feedback?

- **How will you design your legacy?** At the end of your life, when those left behind reflect on your contribution to your community, company, team, and society, what do you want them to say was your legacy? What difference did you make? Did you live authentically and let people know what you valued and believed?

Start Your Authenticity Today

Authenticity requires great introspection and humility. No one is perfect —we are all flawed. We also cannot turn the clock back and undo mistakes (or inauthentic behaviors) from the past.

We can, however, move forward and make changes RIGHT NOW to live more authentically. Focus on being genuine. Stop listening to the scripts of what you should do/believe/want/love/think, and listen to that quiet voice in your heart that knows what is right for you, above all.

Another way you can learn more about your current personal brand is to compare your brand to others'. What brands do you feel a similarity or affinity with? For instance, you might say, "Neiman Marcus is about status and exclusivity, and so am I," or "Ferrari is elegant and fast moving, and so am I," or "Walmart is about being friendly, approachable, and full of value, and so am I." Spend a moment and think about some brands that you relate to and how those qualities, characteristics and traits in yourself align with those brands.

For some people, the current brand descriptive words just roll off the tips of their tongues. They have a clear sense of what differentiates them. For others, it's tough to get to five key words. Whether this was easy or difficult, your key words become a part of how you will project and articulate your value, so it is important to keep working on them until you feel they are right. Remember, too, that personal branding is a journey, and it takes time and practice to build momentum.

Ask Yourself:

What drives and motivates me?

_____

_____

_____

_____

What can I do to help others see my value?

_____

_____

_____

_____

Key Takeaways:

- Your current brand is how you see yourself, how you are, and how others perceive you.

- To help understand your current brand:

  - Compare yourself to other brands you admire and relate to, and determine which qualities in you align with those brands.
  - Understand what you offer the world that is unique from what others offer.

Chapter 12:

Articulating Your Desired Brand

Now that we have an idea of what your current brand is, we need to think about your desired brand. For some of you, your current brand is exactly what you want people to be thinking about you. In that case, you may simply need to get more creative on how you market yourself to remain relevant and compelling. For others, though, your current brand and what you want to be known for don't match. In those cases, we really need to think about and identify a desired brand—your legacy.

As you began to separate from service, think back to your vision—how did you see yourself next? Did you have a goal for the type of work you wanted to do on the civilian side? Did you envision owning your own business or being in charge of a large staff? Did you see yourself working independently or as part of a team? Did you want to use the skills you learned in the military in a career on the civilian side?

How you ultimately want others to perceive (see) you, and the value they will assign you, starts with you. YOU get to set the vision and the direction of your ultimate reputation, and others will learn to experience you this way. This is how it works for everyone—celebrities, politicians, business professionals, and students. Setting the intention and goal of the reputation you want to earn, and acting consistent with that brand, is how you influence the perceptions others have of you.

In clarifying your desired brand, you will begin to articulate your purpose. This purpose is your guide and filter for how/where/and with whom you want to be seen. What do you believe is the reason you are here? Why were you put into this life, in this way, at this time? How would you like your legacy to look?

Exercise

Here's a fun way to get started: Think about how you would like others to see you and feel about you, and answer these questions:

If you were a car, what kind of car would you want to be? Would you be a sexy sports car? Would you be a high-powered big truck? Would you be a family passenger van? And why?

_____

_____

_____

_____

If you were a song, what kind of song would you want to be? Would you want to be a classic melody or a fast-paced, aggressive, heavy metal number? Would there be words in your song, or would it just be melody?

_____

_____

_____

_____

If you were a beverage, what kind of beverage would you want to be? Would you be an energy drink? Would you be a fancy Starbucks drink? Would you be an alcoholic beverage? Would you be a kid's juice drink?

_____

_____

_____

_____

These questions are fun and whimsical, but they're also important in giving you a sense of how you would like to project yourself. Are you a fast race car and a high-energy-drink-type person? Do you see yourself more as a family sedan, maybe a non-alcoholic, non-caffeinated beverage that plays to a melody that's a little bit more traditional? This exercise helps you get a sense of your desired personal brand and your style.

Your Ultimate Legacy

Another way to think about your desired personal brand is to think about the end. How do you want to be remembered? Imagine we're at your funeral, and people who have loved you, worked with you, and known you casually surround us. What would you like these people to say about the difference you made? How do you want them to remember you? What emotions do you want them to experience as they remember your life and contribution? You might want them to say things such as:

"He gave one hundred percent of himself to everything he did ..."
"She made those around her feel welcomed, valued, and loved ..."
"He was a great father and husband ..."
"He could always be counted on in a pinch ..."
"She was the best (fill in the blank) I ever knew ..."

Often, in working with veterans, I hear them describe their current brands this way: "My current reputation is my ability to execute on a strategic and highly classified plan, create dynamic teams that perform at ultimate levels of success ..." Then, when we get to their desired brand and this exercise, they get quiet. They say they want to be known as "a good dad." Or I hear something such as, "You know, I want my team to feel like I was always there for them, that I always had their backs." All of a sudden, we start to hear authentic emotional qualities come through. Remember that branding is about emotions and having your audience feel a certain way about you.

When you look over the list of things that you want to be remembered for, I encourage you to really focus in on the emotional words, the ones that create feelings rather than words that are tactical or strategic or have dollar amounts tied to them. For example, you might choose words like:

loyal	dedicated	empathetic
passionate	creative	honest
resilient	high integrity	proactive

Be sure they describe you, the ultimate you. If you try to create a brand around words and values that are not authentic, you will simply be promoting a myth of who you are. This causes more confusion than good. Focus on feelings-oriented words that truly describe what is in your head and your heart.

Now, take those words, feelings, and thoughts and write five key words that reflect your desired brand. They may be the same five words that you wrote for your current brand, or they might be different. How do you want to be remembered?

My desired brand keywords:

1. _____

2. _____

3. _____

4. _____

5. _____

How does that feel? It's tough, yes! We're getting really close to figuring out your personal brand—what makes you unique and what strengths you have. You might already be seeing some patterns jump off the page!

We will use these keywords as we move forward in building your personal brand. You have now set an intention of how you would ultimately like to be remembered. This is a powerful step! It's ok to change these keywords later if a better word comes to you. Remember, this is YOUR process. You will make it work for you, in a fluid and authentic way.

Example:

Bob is, by all accounts, one of the nicest people you'll ever meet. He is warm, approachable, hospitable, and personable. Everyone knows Bob as a "nice guy."

Bob is also CEO of a highly successful technology company that serves children in the education system. Bob is deeply passionate about innovation and is schooled and versed in education technology. He has committed his life to improving the education system in the U.S. and has created numerous technologies and systems currently in place. But at the time his public relations team hired me to help, he wasn't credited with many of them.

The problem was that being known as a "nice guy" didn't reflect what he had accomplished and what made him credible as a formidable "thought leader" in his field.

In redirecting Bob's reputation beyond "nice guy," he and I began with a deep inventory of his brand assets, the things he has done that make him credible as a thought leader in the education industry. After a personal brand audit and brand feedback assessment, we identified specific and compelling opportunities to broaden his exposure, fine-tune his audience focus, and begin to target his personal brand in a more intentional way.

The game plan we developed included creating a new vernacular for him to use to articulate his thoughts and position. For instance, I directed him to speak of his work with terminology that could articulate his vision for "disruptive" and innovative technology (i.e., using words like innovative systems instead of processes), elevate his stature, and clue in the audience that he is introducing new concepts, not simply advancing the status quo. While his audience of educators needed to warm up to this new language, they took note of the bold and elevated way he now discussed his vision for change. They noted his increased confidence and the more impressive way he presented himself.

His audience began to see his passion, appearance, tone, and style as that of a thought leader and not just a colleague they enjoyed being with. A key moment came for Bob at a large education conference he attended along with peers, vendors, industry leaders, and his staff. During a general session presentation, a speaker whom Bob greatly respects pointed to him from the stage and said to the audience of several hundred people, "There, my friends, is a true visionary in our field!" Bob knew then that his personal brand was finally being recognized.

Bob is still a very nice person—the kind of man you'd be fortunate to know and even more fortunate to work with—but he is also becoming known for his expertise, passion, and commitment to education technology. He is a sought-after speaker at international events where thought leaders gather. Most important to Bob, he is able to broaden his voice in advocating for education reform and innovation, which is his true calling.

Ask Yourself:

How do I want people to feel about me?

_____

_____

_____

_____

What do I want my legacy to look like?

_____

_____

_____

_____

What will I be most remembered for?

_____

_____

_____

_____

Am I living the way I need to live in order to have that legacy?

_____

_____

_____

_____

Key Takeaways:

- Your desired brand is the legacy you hope to leave after you're gone. This legacy is set in your reputation and the connections and experiences others had with you when you were alive.

- To help determine your desired brand:

  - Think of how you want people to remember you after you are gone.
  - Formulate your thoughts in terms of feelings and emotions rather than words that are tactical or have dollar amounts tied to them. Branding is about emotions and feelings.

Chapter 13:

Set the Vision of Your Goals

In order to build a meaningful personal brand that attracts the opportunities you desire, from the audiences you will target, it helps to have a clear vision of the goals you seek to achieve. As you consider your goals, give yourself freedom and permission to dream. There is great power in dreaming and vision-setting.

Every recruiter and hiring manager I've spoken with encourages candidates to dream large and shoot high. You may have work you need to do to get there, but if you settle for mediocrity, that's what you'll attract.

Set a vision for your spiritual goals. What do you aspire your spiritual life to be like when you have built a well-defined and meaningful personal brand? How will a healthy soul look to you?

My spiritual goals:

_____

_____

_____

_____

Articulate a vision for your emotional health, too. What will it look like if your relationships are in tact and rewarding? How will you treat yourself and others?

My emotional goals:

_____

_____

_____

_____

Is intellectual growth important to you? Will you pursue life-long learning? What will that look like—advanced degrees? Reading books and journals? Discussing intellectually stimulating topics regularly with others?

My intellectual goals:

_____

_____

_____

_____

Your financial goals are important to write down. What lifestyle do you aspire to achieve? There is no right or wrong answer here—just yours. Put down a number, paint a picture, clip a photograph of a goal you set for what financial success in your vision will look like.

My financial goals:

_____

_____

_____

_____

Being physically healthy is important to be emotionally sound. How will you support your physical health during your life. Will you become expert in a sport, work out at a gym regularly, or exercise independently? How often? Set this vision for yourself.

My physical goals:

_____

_____

_____

_____

Finally, how will you live in community with others? If serving a community of like-minded people is important to you, what will that look like? How will you serve and connect? Are they passionate about veteran issues, health, global crisis or education? Articulate your commitment and vision for this aspect of your life.

My community goals:

_____

_____

_____

_____

Gratitude

In 2013, I had a unique opportunity to get in touch with my vision. I realized it was important for me to truly and wholly trust in my vision for what I was doing... and what I was asking people to believe in with me. I became aware that fear and doubt were starting to creep into my thoughts for the first time in my business. I'd like to share the story with you here, to provide insights and inspiration at this part of your journey. If you would like to read the entire Gratitude Project story, please visit my blog: http://unleashingyourbrand.com/my-gratitude-project/

In 2013 I shared the story of a very personal experience. In no way does it compare to the horrors of war, the trauma of life-threatening disease, or anything of that nature. But, for me, it was a life-changing opportunity to learn about myself, trust, vulnerability, and about the beauty and goodness of other people.

You see, I am that person who walks around incredibly grateful for the things I have, including a loving husband, two amazing adult sons, money in the bank (not a ton, but enough), my health, and living parents who tell me they are proud of me all the time. For some reason, however, I also worry that one day it will not be enough, and I begin doubting myself, as we all do at times. I worry that I may not be enough.

A friend suggested I needed to push myself far outside my comfort zone to get past this fear. She strongly suggested that in order to build full trust in my gratitude and appreciation for the blessings in my life, I should go up to complete strangers (one per day for seven days) and give them an envelope containing a personal note and cash (an agreed upon amount that she and I decided). The note will contain a personal message of gratitude—I will express appreciation for my life, and my gifts and include a wish for the recipient—and will be signed with just my first name. This exercise was not about marketing myself or evangelizing appreciation. Rather, I was going to be authentic and vulnerable and share my gratitude in a very real way with a stranger every day for a week.

I knew this was outside my comfort zone even though I speak to groups of strangers for a living. I am the farthest thing from a shy person, yet I was trembling at the thought of being vulnerable with a stranger over something that is so important to me (gratitude).

For seven days of my life, my mission is to find one person every day (and I "will know who it is supposed to be") with whom to share the message and the note.

Over the week that followed, I was consumed by this exercise. I experienced joy, fear, anxiety, exuberance, questioning, and many answers. I saw myself in others and worried about how these strangers would react to a woman approaching them and offering to hand them a note which they didn't understand. In only one instance did someone refuse my gesture, and I learned from that, too.

I realized that in feeling my gratitude I learned to become so much more other-focused and aware. I was tasked with believing I would know *who* I was supposed to meet and give my note to. That proved challenging itself—what if I chose the wrong person? As I questioned myself more and more, I learned to trust my intuition and instincts. I would "know". Trust.

The seven days were over and my notes were handed out. I know I made a difference in the lives of the people I met and maybe I even inspired some of them to do a similar project. There was the one young girl who took photos of my note and cash and posted it online—maybe her friends would find a way to help someone else some day.

Stepping Outside of Fear

It's now been almost a year since I did my Gratitude Project. Even so, I find myself thinking about the experience often—the fear I felt at the initial suggestion, writing all the notes, the first woman I gave my note to, and the last woman whom I met.

I've decided to share this project with you because I trust that's what I'm supposed to do. Have you ever done something similar? Do you believe in the overwhelming gratitude that can come from random acts of kindness? If you find yourself stressed and troubled with fear over this process, stepping outside of fear—and towards gratitude—can be a powerful motivator and can refocus your energy in a very productive way!

Chapter 14:

The Power of Feedback

Think about your current brand and your desired brand. How close are the two? Do you really know? The best way to assess how close you are to your desired reputation is with honest and reliable feedback.

Let's look at it this way: Have you ever been sitting across the desk from your commander as he begins to share some of the concerns and feelings others have about you? Some of them find you difficult to deal with. Others have commented that you take over meetings. Or maybe your staff feels you don't have their backs and advocate for their needs. We don't always know what others think of us.

My good friend, Olivia (not her real name), had been promoted to senior vice president of a large international company. She was in charge of a national sales team and had been hired in October. In December, the company hosted a holiday party, and her team flew in from across the country to celebrate. For the first time, she met several of the people on her national team in person. Halfway into the party, she walked into the restroom, shut the stall door behind her, and heard two women come in right after her. The first woman said to the second, "Have you met Olivia Owens?"

Hearing her name mentioned, my friend perked up. She thought, "Oh my gosh, I'm going to hear a conversation about me!"

Then the second woman replied to the first, "Yes! I have met Olivia! Who the heck does she think she is?"

Olivia was stunned. As she describes it, she wanted to curl up on the floor and become invisible. She continued to overhear, unbeknownst to her colleagues, a conversation between two executives on her team describing someone they perceived as "stubborn, arrogant, pushy, and exclusive."

But that's not Olivia! Olivia knows herself to be collaborative, engaging, supportive, and yes, driven—but in a good way.

Similarly, I worked with an attorney who should have been on track to become a partner in the firm. However, she repeatedly heard feedback from her colleagues and superiors that she wasn't seen as a "team player." This was frustrating to her, because it kept limiting her opportunities for advancement in the firm. She wasn't included in the partner retreat, and she wasn't invited to happy hour with the other partners, which was typically what they did when they were grooming somebody for a partnership.

We talked about this "team player" feedback. To her, the term team player meant something very different from what it meant to her peers. To her, being a team player meant sitting her team down around a table and saying, "You do this, you do this, you do this, and you do this." That was how she saw team play—clear, direct, and highly functional. The firm had a different vision. The more she perpetuated this behavior and reinforced this reputation, the more limiting it became.

In one of my veteran transition workshops, I asked all of the participants to offer feedback on one of their colleagues, who was participating. These veterans had only known each other a few days, so they really didn't know each other very well. The point of the exercise was to offer feedback to each other that was close to "first impression" feedback, unlike the kind you would receive if someone knew you more intimately.

At first, several of the veterans (all men, by the way) squirmed in their seats. I was asking them to give feedback and input to (almost) strangers and was instructing them to use emotional/feeling words. "How does John make you feel?"

After a few minutes, however, what happened was not surprising—as each person shed light into another participant's personal brand, new information and insights were revealed. They started to really get into the exercise!

One former Marine drill sergeant who stands at a commanding height of 6'6" remarked to me afterwards, "I had no idea that I came across to others as friendly and approachable. I always thought I looked scary and that's why employers didn't want to hire me." This new information empowered him to be even more friendly and social—traits he very much wanted to be known for.

Feedback is an important tool to measure, assess, and test reality against perception. It helps us gauge whether we're close to our desired brand. Many of my clients discover through feedback that their current brand is perceived to be closer to their desired brand than they thought. What a discovery!

Other clients learn of positive traits others see in them that they didn't realize they were bringing to the table. What a gift that knowledge would be!

I have a client, for example, who is a successful female entrepreneur in a high profile but heavily bureaucratic industry. She is also very tall, with striking, naturally red hair. In her mind, her stature and appearance were liabilities since, as she put it, "My look makes an entrance into a room before I do!" However, after receiving personal branding feedback, we learned that her target audiences loved her bold appearance and attributed the impact and success of her message to the forcefulness of her physical presence. She was seen as more passionate, credible, and confident because of this striking appearance. Upon learning this, we were able to weave her appearance into her personal brand marketing strategy in a more direct way. She now feels comfortable leveraging this personal strength more intentionally.

Positive feedback is usually welcome. But too much of a good thing might not be useful in managing your personal brand. A former client of mine, Joe, was a highly decorated TOPGUN pilot in the Navy before retiring twenty years ago to enter the business world. Joe is currently a CEO of an energy company, where his staff is aware of his decorated military past. One concern for Joe is the constant and unexpected heaps of praise his staff gives him, almost constantly. While the praise and compliments are flattering, he has begun to find it uncomfortable and has begun to question the validity of the input. This is an example of too much positive feedback being detrimental. The input certainly doesn't help Joe manage and direct his reputation in productive ways.

Negative feedback, like the kind Olivia (mentioned above) encountered, is just as useful. Imagine you accidentally overheard gossip that reflected negative feelings about you. Maybe you overheard two colleagues complaining about the way you manage meetings or your lack of participation in team activities. What powerful feedback! What a gift! They have alerted you to a perception brewing, and that perception can spread and grow if you don't take action.

Here's another example of feedback and perception from Paul Bogacz, Captain (Ret.), United States Air Force; Curriculum Developer, United States Personnel Professional Development School:

> My first interaction with this Lieutenant Colonel was when she came to my installation as a student to one of my courses. I was in need of immediate assistance from a peer and found him in a side room in conversation with the Lieutenant Colonel. I pardoned myself and, in true True Colors Orange approach, asked my peer for a moment because of some very time-sensitive requirements. The Lieutenant Colonel was stone-faced but, since I didn't know her and since they were in a public area, chatting (my perception) on a break, I thought nothing of pulling my peer aside. Surely she understood I had 30 other students who were depending on me to get my job done.

Later in the week, after I taught a variety of lessons to the group, the Lieutenant Colonel approached me, asking me for a moment. She wanted to apologize to me; claiming she had jumped to a horrible conclusion about me—as a person and professional. She didn't appreciate my high-energy approach from the previous interaction, and after getting to see me in the classroom, experiencing my drive and passion for instruction and student-interaction, and my knowledge of classroom management, she was extremely impressed. She admitted that she had been wrong in her judgment about me. She maintained a relationship with me, offering advice, insight, and guidance ... and even a connection or two. She also offered me a job, if I was interested, when I planned on leaving the military.

How to Solicit Feedback

There are many forms of feedback. In many companies, employees receive regular performance reviews and evaluations as part of their job. Typically, these reviews are structured and directed by the human resources department. They are designed to measure job performance, skills, aptitude on the job, as well as your ability to work well with others and contribute to the company. In some cases, employees are also measured on their leadership skills and potential to grow in the organization.

There are also informal forms of feedback, and we all have access to these. We can have hallway conversations with colleagues or associates. We can take clients out to lunch and ask them about our perceived brand. I just mentioned that gossip could be another form of feedback. I'm not advocating that you pay attention to all water-cooler conversation, but if you overhear gossip, maybe you can spot a pattern in your perceived behavior and detect important insights about your brand. Maybe you can identify roadblocks in your career or relationships that are a result of this perception.

In assessing your personal brand, I encourage you to consider feedback from colleagues, peers, clients (even past clients), staff, direct reports, and associates. Ask yourself: Who do I need to bring in close? Who do I need to get feedback from? Who will give me honest, compelling, relevant information that will allow me to become more effective in building my reputation?

Encouraging Honest Feedback: Building Trust

It isn't always easy to get honest input. We often need to encourage feedback because people withhold it for many reasons. Sometimes, people don't give us their honest opinions because they're afraid they will upset or offend us. Sometimes, they're not sure or confident about their input or maybe they want to avoid conflict. Sometimes, people don't share feedback with us simply because they haven't been asked.

Offering honest feedback can be as difficult for the person giving it as it can be for you to hear it. To feel safe in offering feedback, it's important that the people you approach feel respected and valued and see you as open, trustworthy, and receptive. Respondents need to know that their feedback is welcome and will help you grow. When they feel safe offering feedback, they will be more candid, honest, and forthcoming.

We want honest feedback because that input can offer valuable insight into opportunities and can help us make good decisions.

When soliciting feedback, keep in mind that you receive respect by showing respect. No matter how painful the feedback may feel or how opportunistic you perceive it to be, you need to show appreciation for the input. Somebody took the time to open up his heart and give you feedback that is potentially a gold mine. (Consider how you've felt if you've ever been asked to give feedback that was uncomfortable or painful. You took a chance and opened yourself to another's potential anger. If your feedback is met with disrespect and rage, you are less likely to be forthcoming the next time. Similarly, if the feedback is received in the spirit in which it was offered—to be helpful—then you feel respected and inclined to help again.)

At LIDA360, we remind clients that when receiving feedback, no matter how positive or negative, the most important response is, "thank you." The only way to gain trust and get honest feedback is to acknowledge and treat those who provide feedback—positive or negative—equally. The moment you start rebutting the validity of the feedback—defending your position and perception of yourself—is the moment you begin to destroy trust. We also remind clients to pay attention to the expression on their faces, because even if they're controlling their language and their bodies, their faces tell it all. Remember: People are giving you feedback—it's a gift.

Despite our best efforts to solicit honest feedback, we won't always be successful. In those cases it can be appropriate to solicit anonymous feedback such as with a survey. Many online tools are available where you can see responses in aggregate unattributed (no names attached to responses). Or, you can hire somebody to conduct the feedback portion who can feed it back to you unattributed so you see the responses but not who said what. Anonymous feedback is helpful if you feel that your audience may not be wiling to share comments unless those comments are confidential.

How to Understand Feedback

When you get direct feedback, pay attention to the nonverbal as well as verbal clues that the person offering the feedback is not being completely honest with you. He may not be doing this intentionally; sometimes offering feedback is uncomfortable. You want to pay attention to warning signs such as a change in vocal tonality. Have you ever had a difficult conversation with someone and suddenly her voice got really high? Halting words might also signal a problem: Is the message really difficult for her to articulate? Is there a reason she can't get the words out?

What about ambiguous messages? We often hear the statement "there's truth in jest." What if somebody all of a sudden starts injecting a lot of humor to deflect and defer?

When receiving feedback, also be on the lookout for a sudden change in language usage. My default behavior when I'm sending a direct message to my children is to use their formal names and choose my words very carefully. If the person you're talking to begins choosing very professional language in the discussion, this could be a warning sign that he is struggling to tell you something difficult or possibly trying to cover something up.

Similarly, pay attention to whether someone's words match his body language. For example, say your boss is sharing positive feedback with you on the recent presentation you gave at the board meeting. As he's talking to you, his posture becomes defensive—he crosses his arms, avoids eye contact, perhaps he starts fidgeting with a pen or his hair. Your boss could be struggling with his message, and it would be a missed opportunity to hear only the positive words without noticing that he is also trying to tell you something negative and potentially helpful.

In addition to these concerns, you need to pay close attention to how you are listening to the feedback. Often, we don't hear feedback because we're thinking ahead. If we're thinking ahead, we're missing what the person is saying. As somebody is talking to you, you might be thinking, "Uh-huh, uh-huh, I get it. I got it. I know where you're going, and so I'm already there." However, you might end up coming to a wrong conclusion and miss the opportunity to learn something important and helpful.

Likewise, we often use emotional filters to hear feedback, which can be limiting. We all have emotional filters, predisposed ways of seeing and judging incoming information. We all have preferences, prejudices, or biases to certain people, communication styles, tonality, and body language. We use those beliefs and emotional filters to judge and create a story around what somebody's trying to tell us. For example, if we believe that, "all teenagers exaggerate" or "women talk too much," then our receipt of their information will be clouded, and we could miss important clues. While emotional filters are often our mind's way of being efficient, they can inhibit our ability to listen and hear feedback in its truest form.

Often, we don't listen well because we're striving for our own validation. We're looking for confirmation of our expertise or our beliefs, and we're not hearing what the other person is saying. We're looking for ways their message supports what we believe to be true.

Another reason we might not hear the content of the feedback is because we're protecting ourselves. Our human "fight or flight" instinct tells us to protect ourselves. As your training in the military has taught you, information and intelligence can indicate both opportunity as well as threat. When our defense mechanisms kick in, we refute feedback that we perceive to be harsh, critical, and painful out of self-protection (ego). While this type of reaction is helpful in self-preservation, it's not useful from a personal branding process standpoint: we may miss insight that would help us move toward our desired reputation.

Finally, there's a lot of noise in the world today that can get in the way of our ability to listen constructively to feedback. Between the Internet, cell phones, and busier-than-ever lives, we're easily distracted. This can have a direct impact on the way we receive feedback. We stand no real chance of truly hearing and understanding what somebody's trying to tell us if we're distracted.

Intent is Irrelevant

In receiving and evaluating feedback, you might be inclined to conjecture ideas around the intent or motive of the respondent. Perhaps you're thinking they have an ax to grind or an agenda to promote. Maybe you think they could be trying to steer you in a bad direction. Regardless of how you interpret their feedback, intent doesn't have a lot of relevance. We can't possibly know what someone intends (or is thinking), and second-guessing only diminishes the value of the feedback.

Receiving Disrespectful Feedback

Disrespect is inappropriate, unfair criticism. For example, it's fair for someone to tell you, "I believe you take over meetings" but not to tell you, "You should sit in the back of the room and shut up!" You should never be put in a position in which the feedback you receive causes you to feel like a doormat. If you have asked for genuine feedback from someone and he offers disrespectful, non-constructive criticism, a response from you might be, "I appreciate your input. I'm not sure I agree, but I will certainly give it consideration." This could diffuse a volatile situation and might cause the respondent to reconsider the negativity of his comments going forward.

Think About What Kind of Feedback You Need

At this point, you can start crafting your own feedback game plan. Think about the type of feedback you want to solicit and whether it's business or personal. What feedback on your brand do you think you need at this point? Maybe you're trying to gauge if your current brand is close to your desired brand. Maybe you're trying to find out what your brand looks like to others.

What feedback are you looking for at work and in your personal life?

Here are some simple brand evaluation questions you could email to eight or ten of your clients, peers, colleagues, and maybe even some staff:

"Do I have a personal brand, and if so, what is that brand?"
"If you referred me to someone, how would you introduce me?"
"When you think of me, what special traits do you believe I have?"

Questions like these assess perception: What are you known for? What is your reputation?

Whenever I receive a referral, the first question I ask is, "What were you told about me?" It is important to me to understand how I am perceived in the marketplace. What are people saying about my brand? How are they introducing me? The question, "Would you refer me to somebody else, and if so, how would you introduce me?" provides critical insight into your brand.

Asking "What do you see as my competitive advantage?" might uncover strengths you didn't know you had. Then follow up with the question: "How do you know that? What do I do that makes you say that?" You are not asking someone to tell you if you are a valuable person. Rather, you want to know if she believes you have the ability to build credibility for a competitive advantage and how she would differentiate you. This helps you gauge the distance between your current and desired brands.

Once you have solicited feedback from others, be sure to keep them in the loop. Let them know you are on a personal brand journey and touch base with them in six months or a year. Let them know about your progress and what you're doing to affect positive change. Thank them for their insight.

Debriefing: Feedback After a Loss

No one likes to lose. Whether it's a job, an interview, a project or a relationship, losing is hard.

I remember when I experienced the loss of a prime project I was competing for. My company seemed like an ideal solution to this group's need to rebrand the organization in a real, authentic ,and robust way. We understood the industry, we were well versed on the protocols and strategies needed to succeed, and the target audience was very familiar to us. Our proposal was thorough and in depth; we made sure to highlight emotional qualities to demonstrate our experience and knowledge of the subject matter and core constituencies. But the contract went to another firm. Shucks!

While disappointing, I also saw this as an opportunity to learn. What were their deciding factors? Was there something we neglected to address? Was it "chemistry" with our team? How important was price? I scheduled a phone call with the decision maker, and her input was revealing: It was a close decision (whew!), and we were a very strong contender. The winning team did a better job of articulating a set methodology that gave the client a higher comfort level. Ok, we can understand that. Using a set formula and sticking with an ironclad methodology is not our strong suite. We prefer a process that is documented, yet fluid, and that was not attractive to them. I was glad to learn this information—we could have second-guessed ourselves for weeks otherwise.

Often, when we lose out on something, we forget about the power of feedback. Feedback on our strengths and our weaknesses can shine a light on areas we can improve and can show us those areas where we are more resolve in our value. In this case, we were pleased that the feedback reflected an area we would not have been willing to go deeper on—creating more formal structure has not been key to our success with clients—and the client did a great job of identifying that formal structure was something they needed to feel comfortable. In effect, not getting this assignment was a win-win for all involved.

In addition, the client made it very clear that they would like to keep in touch for future work. While the re-branding might not be our project, they saw other opportunities where our strengths could add value to their team (where our fluid and intuitive process could help them grow and become more profitable).

Next time you lose a contract, a job interview, or a key project, try asking for feedback. Here are some of the questions we asked in this case, which might be helpful to you:

- Was there something missing, incomplete on my application, or not addressed in my interview?
- What were the deciding criteria that helped your team choose?
- Was there something I could have highlighted better in presenting my experience and expertise, particularly my military experience?
- Did my passion for the position come through?
- Was salary a determining factor?
- May I keep in touch with you?

Personal Branding is Not About Changing Who You Are

This personal branding journey you're on is not about changing you, and it's not about changing other people. You can influence, you can affect, you can even manipulate other people, but you can't literally change them.

EXHIBIT A:

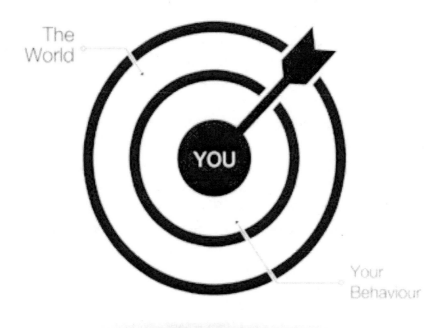

It's important to understand what you actually have control over. The graphic (Exhibit A) helps us understand many things about control. At the center of the circle is where you are. You are set there. You cannot unwind or undo everything that has ever happened to you before you began reading this information. Your DNA, experiences, opportunities, challenges, and gifts are all set at the moment you began this personal branding journey. That's all in the past. Neither you nor I can go back and change them. Likewise, the outer circle represents the world that, like you, can't change how it is wired. You can't change other people nor can you change the way the world is.

What you can control and affect is the band in the middle, which is your behavior. Where you interact with the world, where you come into contact with other people is where perception is formed. The more times you act a certain way, the more often the world—other people—will form perceptions about you based on how they feel about that behavior.

You might receive feedback that causes you to think, "I'm hearing that I'm not a team player" or "I'm getting feedback that says I'm not approachable." These are perceptions you can change through your behavior. One of the changes you might make if you are getting that feedback would be to leave your office door open more often. Or you might look at your personal style: Do you appear closed off and distant? Maybe you dress more formally than the rest of your team and colleagues. You might look at the way you are communicating with your staff. Are you using overly formal language, or do they see your casual side, too?

I met a woman a few years back in one of my programs who was probably in her early twenties. She came up to me after my program and said, "I've got this brand at work as 'the office mom.' Everybody calls me the office mom, and I get feedback that I'm valued because I'm the office mom." But she continued, "I'm getting passed up for promotions. I don't even think I'm getting any respect, because I have this brand, this label." Being known as "the office mom" was clearly hindering her opportunities.

We talked about what she had been doing to build that reputation. In fact, she'd been feeding right into it! She was the person who organized the Friday afternoon parties. She was the one who always set up the meetings with the napkins and the coffee pot and the bottled waters. She was the one who cleaned up afterwards. She was the one who made sure everybody got a birthday card on his or her birthday. She was a very giving, generous, warm person, but because she was feeding into this perception, she was limiting her opportunities. So she had to pull back. It didn't mean she went from being a warm, generous, approachable person to being cold and distant. She didn't change her identity or ignore the experiences in her past that led her to want to be so giving. But she had to remove that brand perception because otherwise, she was not going to be taken seriously and advance in the organization.

Similarly, the female attorney who was not considered a "team player" re-evaluated her behavior to make a positive change and attract her desired opportunities. We developed concrete actions she could use to promote her brand assets and changed the way she interacted with her team and colleagues. For instance, she didn't always speak up at meetings; she let other people have the spotlight. She began asking more questions rather than offering answers. We used her feedback to guide her behavior and build up her reputation and credibility within the firm. She eventually did make partner, because the partners saw her as more apt to be a team player and to be moving in a direction that would grow the firm, her staff, and the values of the firm.

As you craft your feedback strategy, consider the areas that you'll act on as they align with your values. I'm not going to change who I am; I'm not going to change my beliefs; I can't change my DNA; and I'm not going to change my values or those qualities that make me authentic. But I am going to make changes in my behavior to get closer to my desired brand. As I craft and communicate my personal brand, my objective is to create consistent messaging that's compelling and unique to the audiences who can assign me value and provide me with opportunity.

Ask Yourself:

What feedback would I like to receive about my brand and reputation?

_____

_____

_____

_____

What feedback would I act on and what would I ignore?

_____

_____

_____

_____

Who do I trust to give me honest and candid input?

_____

_____

_____

_____

Key Takeaways:

- Feedback is always a gift. Because your goal is to move from your current reputation toward your desired brand, you need feedback to gauge how far you are from your desired brand.

- Solicit feedback on your personal brand by asking people you trust, "Do I have a personal brand, and if so, what is it?" Or "When you think of me, what special traits do you think I possess?" Look for patterns in the responses.

- When receiving feedback, pay attention to both the verbal and nonverbal cues of the people offering it. Look for signs that what they are saying might not be consistent with what they mean, such as:

  - Change of vocal tonality
  - Halting words
  - Sudden change in language usage
  - Words not matching body language

- Avoid these common roadblocks when receiving feedback:

  - Not paying attention and thinking ahead instead of actually listening to what the person is saying
  - Putting the feedback through an emotional filter
  - Striving for your own validation
  - Getting defensive

- Letting modern distractions, such as cell phones, interfere with your ability to hear what's being said

- The intent of the speaker doesn't have relevance when it comes to receiving feedback, because we can't possibly know what others intend.

- Personal branding involves making changes based on the feedback you receive to get you closer to your desired brand; it does not mean changing who you are.

- Always show appreciation for feedback. This will keep the flow of information coming to you.

Chapter 15:

Writing Your Brand Promise

The next step is for you to write your brand promise. A brand promise is not a marketing statement; it's not a tag line; and it's not a slogan. It's a very personal statement that will help guide you through living your personal brand with intention and move you in the direction of your desired personal brand by writing down what you want to be known for. Your efforts toward target audiences, image, marketing identity, and online branding will all filter through your brand promise.

Your brand promise should look something like this:

"In order to be known as __(your desired reputation)____, I will behave this way: __(your behavior, actions, attitude)_____; and I will show that I am authentic in this way: ____(how you will let people see you as real, genuine)_____. I will know my brand promise is working when I see this: ____(benefits, goals you hope to achieve)_____.

We'll approach this in steps, starting with "in order to be known for ..." This is where you'll write your desired brand. Ultimately, what is the reputation you're creating for yourself? Think about your desired brand keywords.

Next, think about how you will behave around others. If you are a human resources professional and your desired brand is to be known as approachable, warm, and compassionate, how will you act on the job? Will you make good eye contact? If you want to be known as approachable and trustworthy, you might demonstrate authenticity by sharing some of your personal stories to make yourself relatable. You might place framed photos of your family in your office so colleagues and staff can learn more about your personal life.

If you are an IT specialist and want to be perceived as innovative and collaborative, you will want to be sure that your body language makes people feel you're approachable and inclusive. You will bring new ideas to discussions and be risk tolerant (innovation). Your brand promise helps to guide your actions, behavior, and communications to build your desired brand.

Similarly, how will you demonstrate your authentic, genuine self to draw others to you? Using the example of the HR professional, you might share stories of your own attempts at career advancement and how they worked out for you. Those might be ways that you can show people who you really are.

Your brand promise is a critical piece of your personal brand development. I encourage you to continually spend time on this. Let it evolve. As you live and work through the promise of how you will be, your identity will begin to flourish. Your personal brand will become the filter through which you will make decisions.

I've had clients turn their brand promises into their computer screen savers (for example, "Always treat others with respect and kindness"). One of my clients wrote hers—"I will strive for inclusivity and collaboration and will not hold onto information or beliefs if they can benefit others"—on an index card and taped it to the steering wheel in her car so that every time she was going to a meeting or out and about, she reminded herself, "This is what I'm working toward, and this is how I need to show up. I need to constantly remind myself what I'm striving for. My brand is a gift."

Example:

In order to be known as someone who is passionate about helping veterans, who is generous, spirited, and ethical, I will behave this way: 1. I will make sure that my work includes ways to help veterans find work; 2. I will give more than I ask... and say "yes" to opportunities often; and 3. I will show up with a smile, bringing optimism to my projects and work; and I will show that I am authentic in this way. I will ask questions when I have them; I will say, "I don't know" if that's the right answer—then I will go find out! I will make sure I look people squarely in the eye and give myself genuinely in my work. I will know my brand promise is working when I see this: When I become a sought-after resource for veterans in transition, when others benefit from my work and talents, and when I feel satisfied that I have given my best in every situation.

Write Your Brand Promise:

In order to be known as _____,
I will behave this way: _____;
and I will show that I am authentic in this way: _____
_____. I will know my brand promise is working
when I see this:_____
_____.

Ask Yourself:

What is my promise to others?

_____

_____

_____

_____

How will I know my brand promise is working?

_____

_____

_____

_____

Key Takeaways:

- Your brand promise is not a marketing slogan. It is a very
  statement of identity and belief and is personal to you.

- A brand promise will help guide you to live your personal brand with intention and move you toward your desired brand. It provides you a roadmap for your personal and professional life.

- A brand promise includes the following pieces:

  - Your desired brand qualities
  - The behavior, actions, and attitudes you intend to display in carrying out your brand promise
  - The ways you will let people see you as real, genuine, and authentic
  - The benefits and goals you hope to achieve

Chapter 16:

Understanding Your Target Audience

If you were a company, like BMW, could you reasonably and effectively market your product to EVERY human being on the planet? No.

Could you reasonably and effectively market your product to every person in the United States? No.

What about every person who drives a car? Still no. It would be financially unreasonable and very ineffective to try to market the assets and attributes of a BMW (sexy, status, high performance, German engineering, etc.) to every person who drives a car: some people don't appreciate those assets; some drivers want something that won't tempt them to speed; others seek a more "family-oriented" car; and still others prefer a car that's lower profile and more unassuming.

BMW, as a company, focuses its marketing on those consumers (drivers and prospective drivers) who find their brand assets attractive and compelling. These drivers perceive value in the BMW brand and will pay more for it—just to experience the expectation of feelings they associate

136

with BMW ("I will feel more powerful... my neighbors will see me as successful...").

For many of you who have spent much of your adult life around the same type of people, in a military setting, determining your target audience might feel like a challenge. The military fosters an environment of various personalities and interests, but the expression of those unique and sometimes disparate views is sometimes stuffed by cultural expectations.

"The military is all about vectoring people towards leadership positions, even though not everyone will be an effective leader," notes Paul Bogacz. "Some people are comfortable with that and it shows in their performance, since that's all they've known for 15 years. However, when they step into the civilian world, they don't know who they are and how that leadership-less brand affects their ability to target a specific audience."

Knowing which audiences you should target is critical to marketing your personal brand. You can't be relevant to everyone out there. Not every potential employer, client, vendor, teammate, or employee will love you or want to work with you. While this might be disappointing to hear, it is real and true.

Instead of spending your time and energy trying to position yourself as interesting/funny/compelling/relevant/valuable to every company that has a job opening, focus on the people and companies who align with you and your values. Look for employers who will find your experience and training valuable, who want to work with you, and with whom you want to work. Similar to BMW, find those target audiences with whom you share the same interests, values, and goals. This reduces the amount of energy and time you will spend positioning yourself and increases the likelihood that you will get noticed for the value you bring to the situation.

Consider: Do you want to work with people who share a military background? Do you work best with people who like structure and rules? Or, do you like to work with creative types, who "go with the flow" and don't hold too much importance in rules?

Your target audiences will be the employers, clients, colleagues, employees, and peers who can offer you opportunities or things of value to advance your career.

Look back at the questions I posed in Chapter 12: If you were a car, what kind of car would you be? If you were a song, what kind of song would you be? If you were a beverage, what kind of beverage would you be and why?

Now, consider if your target audience was a car, what kind of car would it be? If your target audience was a song, what kind of song would it be and why? Finally, what kind of beverage would your target audience be? Would it be a nice, chilled chardonnay or an energy drink? Would it be a cold glass of milk? Why?

Ideally, your responses to your questions and those of your target audience would be the same or very similar. You might see yourself as a Mercedes, and your ideal employer would be a Lexus. You would be a hard rock song, and your preferred employer would be heavy metal.

You would be an energy drink, and your employer would be a strong cup of coffee.

We should target the audience that finds us relevant: the audience that gets our jokes, appreciates our experiences, and values what makes us unique. Your target audience is looking for you, and I can tell you through years of experience that when you find that sweet spot—when you locate the audience that will find you relevant and compelling—things fall into place! Your self-marketing becomes a lot more focused and a lot less costly. You will go from shotgun to laser marketing of your values and value to others.

Who is Your Target Audience?

- Hiring managers at big companies in the energy industry?
- Employers who seek a military intelligence background?
- Professionals who lack leadership skills and need training?
- Companies craving someone to bring integrity, hard work, and ethics to the workplace?

My Target Audience is:

_____

_____

_____

_____

Researching Your Audience

Once you've identified a target audience, it's important to understand everything you can about who they are and what they like, because your goal is to show yourself as relevant to solving their problems and meeting their needs. If you don't know much about them, they might all blur together in your mind and appear all the same. Or, you risk trying to appeal to them in ways they can't understand and relate to. Imagine trying to talk about leadership and integrity (strong skills gained in military service) to an employer who wants you to hide receipts "off the books."

At the same time, you will have to be mindful to not change who you are to become relevant. I am not suggesting you alter your personal brand and identity to fit this audience's needs. You shouldn't have to. I recognize that sometimes it feels easier to pretend to be someone you're not or someone you think others expect you to be. This is not authentic. While you might have to project more confidence or self-esteem than you feel at that specific moment (such as in a job interview), you should strive to remain genuine at all times. During your military service you may have had to implement strategies of projecting a persona for survival; in the civilian world that will be harder to maintain on a consistent basis, particularly given the relationships you will form on the job.

I worked with a client in California who was in the financial planning profession, and she was passionate about technology. She was in her late twenties, a very bright young woman who loved all things technical. She managed all her appointment data through her iPhone; she emailed webinar invitations; she emailed client newsletters, alerts, and feedback surveys; she utilized technology in the most robust ways possible. She invested a lot of time and energy into understanding her field, developing her skills, and using technology to communicate her value to clients and prospects.

Interestingly, however, her target audience was composed of couples currently in retirement. These weren't people in their forties or even fifties. They were mostly seniors in their sixties, seventies, and beyond. That was her sweet spot, and she heavily relied on technology to communicate with and market to them.

The "open rates" on her emails were terrible; her feedback surveys came back with hardly any responses. Her marketing wasn't reaching its target, and it was obvious she hadn't studied her audience, who wasn't comfortable with technology. They were terrified to close their computers at night because they were afraid all their information would be gone in the morning. She was using the wrong marketing to get to the right audience. Once she better understood her audience and started doing more traditional marketing—phone calls, stopping by, direct mail —her client response rates and engagements skyrocketed.

In doing the "car, song, beverage" exercise, Richard, one of my executive clients said that if he were a car, he would be a NASCAR race car. He would be built for one time around the track; he would be all about speed—few gears, all about action! If he were a song, he would be heavy metal. If he were a beverage, he would be the highest-octane energy drink you could imagine. Then we began narrowing his target audience, and he told me that his audience would be an old Volkswagen bug from the 1960s with the big flower stickers on it. If his audience were a song, it would be a classic American pop song. If it were a beverage, he said it would be milk. Those were his answers! You can see where there might be some confusion and misalignment in how he relates to his audience.

Richard understood that he had a challenging situation in front of him: Would he change his target audience (to a group more easily suited to his style and personality) or would he change his behavior? He made the choice to change some of his behavior to communicate the values of his brand, because he and his audiences were speaking different languages and living different styles. There was an opportunity to build better rapport, to gain deeper relationships, and to create champions for his cause if he was willing to make some behavioral modifications. Seeing this as advantageous to his career and reputation, he made the conscious choice to make changes. He was not changing who he was, just changing how he was.

Richard began taking slower strides when walking into a room to meet these clients. He talked more slowly to ensure they heard every word. He leveraged his energy and passion in ways that his audience could relate to (e.g., he spoke about their common mission, engaging this audience in the cause) and not in ways that would cause them to recoil. Just because his audience was not aligned in behavior to him did not mean he needed to find another audience or reinvent himself to be relevant. He was in control of how his behavior influenced and affected that audience, and he made the choice to modify his behavior to be more approachable to and engaged with this target group. Making such a choice is always in your control; it is your option.

Think about your behavior and your target audiences. What happens when you describe your military duties to a hiring manager with no military experience? Do her eyes glaze over... or worse, does she imagine the horrific images she's seen in the movies? Is your energy level overwhelming to your prospects? Do they recoil from your intensity and energy? Or, as you describe your passion for the industry and share relevant experiences, are their eyes widening and are they starting to sit forward—drawn to you because they can relate to you, your behavior, language, and beliefs?

Study your target audience carefully. What do you know about them: Do they embrace technology? Do they seek efficiency, or do they want to have intimate conversations? You will need to make sure that you're responding to your audience's needs. What do they want, and what will motivate them? Who else is influencing this audience? Are they active in social media? Are there groups they participate in?

Learn as much as you can about what motivates and influences your audience. You can easily find a lot of information online done by others who may be targeting your same audience. If you're looking to target the millennial generation, for instance, there are numerous papers, books, and other tools to help you gain understanding about that audience.

And don't forget to research where your target audience hangs out, as well. Are they active online? What type of groups do they belong to? Do they hang out in industry associations? This will help you once you begin your marketing and networking efforts. Your goal is to find opportunity to cross paths and start a dialog. Then, you can build visibility for your personal brand and get noticed by the right people.

When You Are in Conflict With Your Audience

When you are not clicking with the audiences that you are trying to align with, you feel out of sorts. This often shows up as feeling "outside" or "left out" of jokes, conversations, and issues that are important to you.

During your service, you most likely aligned with the values of your fellow service members. You focused on a similar mission and goals and brought consistent values and beliefs to each situation. However, if your personal brand conflicts with the values of the organization or company you work for, that could be why your stomach has been hurting. Whether your work is in the area of environmental sustainability, health care, or interior design, it's important that your personal brand support that effort, or it will reveal a big disconnect. When your values, competencies, and goals are not supported or in line with those of the people you work with, you feel misaligned.

Your Audience has Functional and Emotional Needs

As you learn more about your audience, it is important that you focus on more than their functional needs. Most of us are really good at knowing the functional needs of our audience, the requirements that make us even a distinct possibility to them. Hiring managers look at a resume to make sure the candidates have the required skills, core competences, technical aptitude, education, and work experience. Functional needs are the attributes and characteristics that we need to meet the minimum standard for consideration. You will often find functional needs spelled out in Requests for Proposals (RFPs) and on job descriptions.

Many of us focus on meeting our audience's functional needs by producing resumes and listing bullet points of our expertise on business cards and brochures, showing how we can meet expectations and fulfill goals. If your audience needs IT management, sales, real estate representation, advertising exposure, or market research, these are the ways you clearly articulate that you know how to do this. These are things an audience needs to check off before you're even part of the conversation. If you don't meet these needs, there's no point in talking further.

Ask Yourself:

What does my target audience need from me (functionally)?

_____

_____

_____

_____

If you only address these functional needs, you will find yourself at a great disadvantage. Audiences also have emotional needs, and these are just as important as (if not more important than) their functional needs.

A hiring manager, for example, will make sure you have the proper expertise and skills to fill a job, but they will also assess whether they feel you will be a good team player and fit in with the group (the company "culture"). Are you someone the rest of the staff would enjoy working with? Will you make me feel good about my decision to hire you?

When you think about the emotional needs of your audience, ask yourself: What does my audience need to feel from me? Does my target audience need to feel that they're going to be treated special? Will they be attended to and cared for as valued clients?

A few years ago I worked with Susan (not her real name), a retired Army Colonel. She told me a revealing story that happened to her while running drills one day. Her commander was screaming at her and her fellow troops in an effort to motivate them into higher performance. The verbal assaults turned into berating, and Susan became increasingly nervous and upset. Suddenly, the commander turned to Susan, looked her square in the eyes and matter-of-factly stated, "I KNOW you want this!" Instead of screaming, she related to Susan in the manner she needed—plain and simple and to the heart. Susan's commander knew what motivated each of her troops and spoke the language they needed to be motivated into action.

When I began consulting and coaching executives on personal branding and reputation management, I mistakenly focused primarily on meeting their functional needs. I believed they expected me to bring project outlines and strategic plans and show them how to properly assess and implement a reputation management protocol that would mitigate risk and manage reward. I produced documents, charts, PowerPoint slides, and spreadsheets highlighting my work and believed that was what they needed to find me relevant and compelling enough to want to work with.

While it is true that my clients need to see methodology and tangible deliverables, they also have very real emotional needs as well. When I learned to recognize and respond to the emotional needs of my clients—

their need to feel safe, validated, appreciated, cared for, and inspired—I became a very effective resource and guide to them. My value and worth to my clients went from "delivering strategic plans and reputation management tools" to being a trusted advisor in their most important decisions. That is the place I am happiest working—where I do my BEST work—and where my fee is more closely aligned with the needs of the marketplace.

Relating to Your Audience: Translate Your Experience

In explaining your relevancy to your audience, you have to do the hard work upfront. Particularly with military veterans I often hear, "hiring managers don't know what to make of my military experience." It is not their job to understand your experience and how that will benefit the position you are applying for—it is your job to make it obvious how your past experience qualifies you for the job. You need to translate and adapt your background, stories, examples, and resume to make it relevant and compelling to your target audience.

Here is a perfect example of how this works: I met Jon, along with several of his colleagues, during a week-long workshop I ran for disabled U.S. veterans in the Wall Street Warfighters Foundation program.

Jon is tall, handsome, and outgoing—a true Texas gentleman. He had been in military intelligence in the Army before being injured and losing a leg in combat. His return to civilian life had been a difficult transition, despite his gregarious and happy personality.

Jon didn't know how to take what he had learned in the service and translate it into a successful job interview. He found it difficult to explain his past career choices, his military experience (much of which is classified), and his goals for a future career. He struggled with sharing too many details of his involvement in the Army or not enough to keep someone interested.

We needed to translate the skills and abilities Jon had learned as a career military officer into relatable and differentiating skills and talents that would attract financial services hiring managers.

First, we took inventory of his work in the service and the way he personally approached that work. His collaboration skills were one particular quality that kept coming up. Jon excelled at team-building and getting buy-in from members of his unit at all levels. Combining his leadership skills, dedication to task, and exceptional education, we articulated his personal brand as a leader, collaborator, and someone people would enjoy working with. We were able to show potential employers what a passionate and accomplished financial professional looked like—one who had valuable collaboration and team-building skills.

Jon recognized that his passion still resides with helping veterans, so today he works with veteran transition programs in Texas.

The world is very busy. People are distracted. Most likely, the audiences you are targeting will be too preoccupied, stressed, and overwhelmed with checklists, projects, and deadlines to spend the necessary time understanding how four deployments in Iraq makes you the perfect fit for a construction management position. You need to spell it out for them by highlighting the responsibilities you held, the roles you played, the tasks you managed, and the people you led, always showing the value-add and benefit you provided. Explain how successes on the battlefield make you a good fit for that company and that position.

Demilitarize Your Experience

Let's say during your years of service you developed a specialty with specific complex weaponry. Depending on the civilian career you are pursuing, that may or may not be relevant to the job. Instead of promoting the technical accomplishment alone, highlight in your resume, elevator speech, and interview how the training and skills needed to successfully operate this weaponry gave you the self-control, patience, and focus needed to be successful in other jobs. Talk about the responsibility for value (weapons are expensive!) and lives that were placed in your care and what that commitment meant to you. Do you have an example of how the skills and talents needed to be a specialist at complex weaponry are helpful to the job for which you are applying? What benefit will you create because you can think well under pressure?

Leverage your military responsibility and explain that the skills you learned in service translate to valuable training for complementary jobs in the civilian sector by pointing out the specific benefits. Connect the dots between your past and your future, and help your audience understand how you make sense in your next position.

Consider Mary, a cook in the United States Navy for 10 years. She ran that kitchen and never missed a beat when it came to serving well-balanced and delicious meals to her crew. When asked about her background, Mary says, "Cooking. It's all I know how to do."

In fact, Mary was responsible for the planning and preparation of nearly thirty meals a week for hundreds of crewmen. She budgeted expenses and managed a tight financial profile of costs and inventory to keep the kitchen running smoothly. Mary knows more than just cooking! When she lists out her experience in broader terms, she becomes more relevant and compelling to a potential employer.

Consider:

- Look through your military resume and find the patterns: Do you work well under pressure? Are you more of a leader or manager? Do you prefer high profile roles or more behind-the-scenes? Do you consistently exceed expectations placed on you?

- Filter your military terminology to make your resume understandable by civilians.

- Understand the needs/goals of the civilian hiring manager. They may or may not understand military scenarios. Help them see that your military career prepared you for the job you are applying to.

- Be yourself. Being authentic and genuine makes you real and relatable. If you don't know an answer in the interview, don't struggle to find an answer. Let the recruiter know that you'll get back to them with the answer. This builds rapport and trust faster than if you try to fake an answer.

If you can meet the emotional needs of your audience, you can create brand attraction. When you talk to prospective employers, you have to focus on their needs—from tactical (job skills and training) to emotional (trust, safety, and validation). Your competitors might be good at producing many of the tangible, functional things your audience needs. But your value proposition—your unique talent—lies in your ability and intuitiveness in meeting your audience's emotional needs as well. This gives you a competitive advantage.

Ask Yourself:

My target audience needs to feel:

_____

_____

_____

_____

Who is Influencing Your Audience?

As you consider the needs of your audience members, also pay attention to who is influencing them. For instance, if your target audience is your direct supervisor, consider who is influencing her. In this case, your peers in the company or team, your direct staff, or even trade publications could be impacting their perception of you. If so, you need to be relevant to these entities, too, as they can help you build your reputation (your personal brand) with your supervisor. If it's important to your boss that you build your brand position as an expert in your field and you know your boss is active in a particular association, for instance, you might choose to write an article highlighting your expertise in that association's magazine. This will raise your profile in business circles and perhaps even more importantly, in your boss's eyes.

Let's say your audience is your potential employer—companies where you are applying and interviewing. Who's influencing them? The media (print, broadcast, and online)? If so, you will need to promote your brand through these outlets via social media. Your staff, company, colleagues, and media presence are extensions of you and must be consistent voices that reflect your differentiation and uniqueness. How we walk the talk is what ultimately builds integrity and credibility.

Ask Yourself:

What do I know about my target audience?

_____

_____

_____

_____

Who is influencing my target audience?

_____

_____

_____

_____

How can I get the attention of my target audience?

_____

_____

Key Takeaways:

- Your target audience is the relevant group you focus on to promote your brand. You can't market yourself to everyone. Focus on the audiences who need to "get" you.

- Pay attention to the functional and emotional needs of your audience. What tangible things do they need to get from you, and what emotional connections or feelings do they need to have about you?

- Focus on being relevant. Demilitarize your resume to highlight how your experience creates a benefit to your next employer.

- Where is your audience hanging out? Maybe they participate in industry events (like meetings of lawyers, doctors, or architects). Are they active in a local chamber of commerce or economic development agency? Where do they gather socially (maybe alumni groups or sporting events)? Once you've found the right audience, you should get to know everything you can about them to show yourself as relevant and compelling. Become intentional about being where your audience is—in person and online.

- Pay attention to who is influencing your target audience, including colleagues, associations, and media. Who has the ear and the attention of the people you want to reach?

Chapter 17:

Understanding Your Competition

To be effective, we can't neglect our competitors. We have to know what they're up to, what they do well, and how they're attracting the attention of our target audience. We can learn from our competitors by taking some of their best practices and seeing if these practices feel natural and authentic to us.

In a job search, your competition might be other applicants or someone currently in the job you're seeking. Working in a job, your competition might come from others who want to do work with your clients/customers, someone at your work who feels threatened by you and wants you out of your job or someone you work with who competes with you for attention, recognition, resources, or more opportunity. Whoever the competitor, you should evaluate and assess them—online, in print, or in person—and pay attention to their actions.

Know their weaknesses, but don't promote yourself by drawing attention to their deficits. I do not advocate building your brand by putting other people down. Highlight your value, show instances where you live consistently with your beliefs, and enjoy the credibility you will develop.

Ask Yourself:

Who is my competition?

_____

_____

_____

_____

What are they missing? Are they skipping some steps? Are they overlooking opportunities that can benefit me?

_____

_____

_____

_____

Are they targeting the same audience as me? If they are, are they targeting it in the same way?

_____

_____

_____

_____

Where do my competitors hang out? Who are they networking with?

_____

_____

_____

_____

Where do my competitors hang out online? What social networks are they using well?

_____

_____

_____

_____

It is important to understand what opportunities your competition is securing and how you can learn their secrets to success.

As I stated above, I do not advocate branding yourself against your competitors (i.e., leveraging their weaknesses in articulating your strengths), but it is important to understand what your competitors are up to. Study them online, learn how they are positioning themselves to the same target audiences you are. Learn what they are offering and how they are capturing the attention of influencers you want to reach as well.

In positioning yourself against your competitors, strive for integrity in how you show yourself to be more compelling and relevant (and a better fit for the job)!

Example:

Instead of saying, "You don't want to hire a non-veteran because they don't know how to handle pressure..."

Say, "When you consider what will make a candidate successful in this job, the ability to manage stress and change seems important. My service taught me how to respond intelligently and effectively when dealing with stress, often when the path is not clear to the team. I would make an excellent employee for that skill and training..."

Key Takeaways:

- Learn from your competition. Watch what they do well and emulate what feels authentic for you.

- Look for opportunities that your competition might be missing. Capitalize on those opportunities to appeal to the same target audience.

- Recognize that your competition might change over time. Keep an open mind, and continue to learn who they are and what they are doing right/wrong.

Chapter 18:

Tying It All Together

Once you've looked at your current and desired brands and have taken note of your target audience and competition, you're ready to begin crafting a strategy to make yourself relevant and compelling to that target audience.

You will look for opportunities to integrate your brand across your relationships and begin thinking about how you live online so you can be consistent in the choices you make. You can now begin to create your own success! One of the greatest benefits from marketing an intentional personal brand is that you attract opportunities. When you take control of your reputation and manage the expectation others have of you, your marketing becomes much more effective and efficient.

Personal branding is about setting the expectation others will have of you. You determine what value, contribution, and reputation you want to have in the minds of your target audience. Other will people have beliefs, biases, and feelings about you and your time in service. It may not be fair, but it's true. You can influence how they perceive you through your behavior and how you communicate your values.

As you craft your strategy, don't forget that you can't rely on personal branding to make you someone you aren't. Your personal brand must stem from your authentic self, your true values. This is why it is so important to understand how you want to be known, because marketing will be the call to action. Branding sets the promise of the experience of working with you.

In the coming chapters, I offer several marketing strategies and tactics for you to consider and act on. I am presenting them with the understanding that if they are right for you, based on your goals and desired brand, they will provide a framework and strategy for you to leverage your personal brand and stand apart from others. Through careful and focused personal branding and marketing, you will enjoy the benefits of greater focus and control over your career, increased visibility, recognition for your accomplishments, and satisfaction in your personal and professional relationships.

Articulate Your Superhero Moment

Think back over your career (in service or outside) or your personal life and remember a time when you felt like a Superhero. Recall a time—and we've all had them—when you accomplished or achieved something, and at the end of that experience you felt completely empowered and invincible, as if you had super powers and could achieve anything! This is a time when you believed you could truly accomplish ANYthing. For many people, superhero moments come from a professional experience; for others, they come from a personal experience.

What were you doing? Who were you with? What contribution did you make that led to the moment for you? Maybe you were part of a mission, a process, or an effort that made you feel so empowered and confident that there was nothing you couldn't do! Did you lead your platoon through a dangerous scenario? Did you stop a high-stakes conversation from spinning out of control? Did you get up to speak in front of a large audience and pull it off flawlessly? Did you help a soldier or friend with a tough decision?

Maybe you were the first one in your family to graduate college? Was getting through Special Forces training a moment when you truly felt empowered with yourself? One Green Beret I worked with shared that during testing, he repeatedly watched others voluntarily fail. They saw no reason to push beyond their limits. He did not. He persevered past what he thought was his breaking point and the result was a sense of self-pride that he remembers vividly today, even though he joined the Special Forces more than 15 years ago.

This is one of the most valuable exercises you can do. I say that from a personal branding standpoint but also from a coaching standpoint. Often we forget that we've had successes. Whatever you recalled earlier, whether it was taking your child to the bus stop for the first day of school, leading your troops to safety, or standing in front of a hundred people to give a speech while you were terrified, doesn't matter. What matters is that you've had that success; you did something that perhaps challenged you, and at the end you owned the responsibility, the accountability, and the outcome.

I worked with a Marine veteran, Geoff, who had served multiple tours in Operation Iraqi Freedom. He was highly decorated from his work in high-profile scenarios. When I asked Geoff about his Superhero Moment, I thought he would be sharing a story about a complex military scenario he had navigated with skill and focus. Instead, Geoff told me about the day he was released from the military hospital after being injured in Kabul and spending six months enduring surgery after surgery to repair his hip and now-missing leg. When he returned home to his young daughters, he explained to them why he now looked different. His girls responded to him by wrapping their little arms around him, burying their faces into his chest and squealing with delight that he was home. He looked different, but he was still their father. In that moment, Geoff realized that his essence—who he is—could not be taken away with his leg. He felt invincible again. He was a father first and foremost.

As Geoff told this story, surrounded by me and his fellow Marines in the workshop they were attending, the other veterans were physically and emotionally moved. They could relate to the simplicity and significance of his story. They confirmed that he truly should have felt like a superhero in that moment.

In his bedroom, Geoff has a photo of his young daughters taken on the day he returned home. I asked him to put the photo in his wallet, instead. This way, he could look at it before going in for a job interview or when a tough call comes in or when he's feeling stressed about a career move. Keeping the photo close by means he can always remind himself of his ability to persevere, overcome, and keep priorities in check.

This exercise helps us define, perhaps, how we see success for ourselves. But more important for our purposes here, it reminds us of those times when we've been to the top of the mountain, emotionally. So whatever you have pinpointed as your Superhero Moment, find something to remind yourself of that experience and your success. Maybe you have the dog tags from someone you served closely with or maybe it was a business card from a company that you started or your enlistment papers. Whatever it is, try to find something that reminds you of your Superhero Moment, and keep it front and center.

Life can get really difficult. So can tapping into your true self and authenticity. Being able to remind yourself that you've had success, confidence, self-empowerment, and possibilities all at your fingertips can remind you that success will come again!

Ask Yourself:

My Superhero Moment was:

_____

_____

_____

_____

I learned about myself:

_____

_____

_____

_____

Key Takeaways:

- Your personal brand gives you direction in your relationships and in the choices you make to promote yourself.

- You can gain control over your reputation and manage the expectations others have of you by being intentional and strategic about marketing your brand.

- Personal branding must integrate your authentic values and not make you into someone you are not.

- Anchoring your personal brand journey in your superhero moments—those times when you did something truly amazing, personally or professionally—is a powerful way to energize yourself.

- Keep mementos of your superhero experiences close at hand. They will remind you of the success and empowerment you've experienced in the past.

"Courage is being scared to death...
and saddling up anyway."
-- John Wayne

PART IV:

Marketing Your Personal Brand

Chapter 19:

Your Elevator Pitch

As you begin to express your personal brand, an effective "elevator pitch" enables you to articulate your value proposition. The term comes from this scenario: if you were to step into an elevator, minding your own business, and a neatly dressed professional person turned to you and asked, "What do you do?" Could you articulate what you do in a compelling and informative way before the elevator doors opened at your floor?

Wikipedia describes the elevator pitch (also called an elevator speech) as how you deliver an overview of your idea, product, or service in 30 seconds or 130 words or fewer.

Elevator Pitch Guidelines

Often we make mistakes in our elevator pitch. We forget to say what our product or service is. We forget to say how we're relevant to the buyers or key stakeholders who should be concerned with our brand. We forget to tell the person who's listening why she should care. Express your enthusiasm and passion in your elevator pitch. Talk about how your work relates to your brand. What makes you special?

I remember attending a large networking event where they asked everybody in the room to give their elevator pitches. About four people in, a woman stood up and said, "I'm with Merrill Lynch, and I'm a broker," and all the people in the room responded, "Hum..." Later, another woman stood up and said, "I help couples achieve their goals and dreams and live the life they were supposed to live, and I work for Edward Jones..."

If you recognize the names of the firms they work for, you know that both women are in the financial services/wealth management field. However, they articulated their value and relevancy through very different elevator pitches. And neither of them really told me how they could be valuable to me, a potential client, or networking source for them. The first woman listed her title, and did so with a great lack of enthusiasm. She missed the opportunity to share something about herself that was interesting and compelling. The second woman created so much mystery around her service that she bored me. I did not clearly understand how she could help me. She was vague and irrelevant to me.

How to Build Your Elevator Pitch

Step 1: What do you do?

It's important to start off your elevator pitch with a clear description of what you do. Begin your elevator pitch by telling me what you do in a succinct and easy-to-understand way. That doesn't mean reading your resume or telling me that you've practiced international trade law for fifteen years—that's what you *did*.

I might start off my elevator pitch by saying, "I own a national marketing and communications firm." Most people know what marketing and communications are, and by being clear, I convey: "I'm not a Subaru mechanic; I'm not a heart surgeon; I'm not a life coach; I'm not an advertising executive. I own a marketing and communications firm." That's very clear.

Example:

One of my clients might start his elevator pitch by saying, "I have the honor of working in the Office of the Chairman of the Joint Chiefs of Staff ..."

Step 2: How do you do it differently?

After you've stated what you do, then move on to explaining how you do your work differently from others in your field. Focus on something about your work or contribution that is unique, compelling, and memorable. What is it about the way you work with clients that's compelling and authentic? What benefits do your clients get from working with you? What do you do for them that your competitors don't or can't?

Then my client might continue, "... and I focus my work on an area I am passionate about—helping communities build capacity for veteran transition and reintegration..." He is differentiating himself and his focus by illustrating the work he does and why it is meaningful to him.

Step 3: Tell a story; share an example

You'll finish your brief elevator pitch by sharing an example or story to illustrate the benefit or impact of your experiences, skills, value, and offer. As human beings, we relate to stories (most of us grew up learning through storytelling). Your story will highlight the benefits of your work, service, or experience in a way that is clear, concise, and relevant.

My elevator pitch continues something like this: "I own a national marketing and communications firm, with a focus on developing strong brands." I would then add something that gives a little more clarity: "My clients are corporations and executives who want to stand out from their competitors and manage their reputations and legacies." (My competitors might say something like, "I help companies drive sales and leverage in-house talent," or "We bring your marketing message into visual alignment to drive business"). Again, I've made it very clear what I do and how I do it. There is no mystery: if you are my target audience and I've made myself compelling to you, you'll want to learn more.

I might say, "I own a national marketing and communications firm, and I start with the brand, because my clients want to stand apart from their competitors. For example, I worked with a man who was in a field where his clients saw all of the technicians at his level as the same, rather than as individuals. When he began to promote his personal brand and his sense of humor through social media, his clients saw him as more than just a 'technician'; they saw him as a personality who contributed to the team."

Example:

My client, in the example above, could finish by saying, ".. for example, I coordinate programs, events, and discussions with local governments, industry partners, and nonprofit organizations," to paint a complete picture of who he is, what he does, and what he's passionate about.

We never want to miss an opportunity to relay the benefits of our brand. While we might use an elevator pitch to talk about some of the features of what we do (i.e., the services we offer) we never want to miss an opportunity to say, "And here's the benefit my clients get," or "Here's the opportunity they have to become better because of my brand interacting with them."

Ask Yourself:

What I do:

_____

_____

_____

_____

How I do it differently:

_____

_____

_____

_____

Story or anecdote to describe my value proposition:

_____

_____

_____

_____

Guidelines for Making Your Elevator Pitch Compelling

An effective elevator pitch always comes from your heart and your head. It must be interesting and intelligent, and it should follow other guidelines, as well. It must:

- Show excitement for your work. If you enjoy what you do and share that excitement in how you talk about your work, you will leave that impression with others.

- Express interest in others. This means you ask about others and their work. Being other-focused makes people find you more approachable.

- Sound natural. Deliver your elevator pitch in your natural style and voice. Authenticity is tremendously attractive!

- Share examples and testimonials. Particularly if your experience was highly complicated, technical, or confidential; offer a story to illustrate what you do and how you do it. Stories help people understand and relate to your work.

- Pay attention to your body language: As you deliver your elevator pitch, pay attention to your handshake, posture, eye contact, and all of your facial expressions. Show your confidence and the attitude of your personal brand by making and holding appropriate eye contact and engaging with a firm handshake. If you miss delivering good eye contact and offer a weak handshake, it could send the message that you lack confidence and enthusiasm. On the other hand, if you look the person in the eye, give a solid and confirming handshake, and smile genuinely, you send the message that you are ready to build rapport. To be seen as a professional who's confident and excited about your work (or potential work), you want to come across as confident and welcoming. Then, it's likely that others will remember your facial expressions and body language and will also remember your message as consistent and compelling.

- Strive to be concise, succinct, and clear in your elevator pitch. If someone is interested in learning more about you, they will ask questions and make positive eye contact to show interest. At a minimum, if you are concise, they will appreciate your clarity and respect for their time.

Your goal is to create a positive impression with others. In some cases, the person you meet may not be looking to meet someone with your skills or experience. That's okay. At least he knows what you do, and you've hopefully made a positive impression. It could be that his colleague or friend is looking for what you offer, and you want to make sure your new contact would be inclined to make that introduction for you.

Next Steps

Let's say you've given a great elevator pitch to a new contact and now you've come to an awkward silence in the conversation. You follow up your pitch by asking your new contact, "So what do you do?" or "Tell me a little bit about yourself," and the conversation still goes nowhere. Maybe she isn't trained in delivering an elevator speech or in engaging in small talk.

If she doesn't give you anything to follow up on or inquire further about, it's safe to ask, "What do you when you aren't working?" You don't need to ask her what she does on the weekends; you don't need to ask her something that could be sensitive or personal. But everybody does something for fun. That's a perfectly safe question to ask somebody after you've made your elevator pitch.

"What brings you to today's meeting?" is another great way to find common ground. "Was it the topic? The location? The speaker?"

You might also ask, "What type of clients do you work with?" Hopefully, the person can articulate what her ideal client looks like. This question may also give her an opening to reciprocate and ask you about your client base. Either way, your goal is to seek common ground in order to build rapport.

Keep in mind that your elevator pitch is where all your brand elements come to life. The more consistent you are in your message, the more you will be remembered and referred.

Remember, brands grow organically; they don't grow overnight. Similarly, elevator pitches take time and practice. Be patient and understand that the tenth time you give your elevator pitch is going to be a lot better than the first time.

Customize Your Pitch to the Audience

The best part of a good elevator pitch is that it provides a foundation for your first meeting with a potential good contact. You will develop a narrative that feels comfortable to you, is focused, and intentional in building your personal brand and creating the perception of you that you desire. Your elevator pitch is also flexible, meaning you can modify and tweak it depending on who you are speaking to.

Example:

- If you are speaking to another veteran or military personnel, your military jargon and acronyms will be understood. You can speak in that language to forge a relationship, even in an elevator pitch.

- If you are addressing a known civilian, you will avoid graphic details or information that could cast you in a negative light.

- If you are speaking to someone in a hiring position or a potential client, you can flex your elevator pitch to address their goals and possible interest.

- If you don't know who the person you are speaking to is (veteran or not?) then you have a default, standard elevator pitch to fall back on.

Key Takeaways:

- An elevator pitch is a succinct description of your idea, product, or service and a quick and effective explanation of how you do your work differently from others. It allows you to promote your personal brand and enables you to articulate your value proposition.

- To deliver a compelling elevator pitch, show excitement for your work. Let your passion shine through. Passion and enthusiasm are contagious!

- Be careful about your use of jargon and acronyms. Avoid too many abbreviations, which might be unfamiliar to a civilian audience.

- Strive to be concise and clear. Make it easy for others to understand what you do and how you do it.

- Deliver your elevator pitch with authenticity. If you show sincerity, others will feel more at ease with you.

- Share examples and testimonials of your past work with clients and the benefits they received from you to paint a mental picture for others.

- Express interest in others. Ask them open-ended questions about their work and interests to draw them out.

- Use good eye contact and deliver your elevator pitch with a firm and appropriate handshake. Effective eye contact and handshakes make a positive impression and reinforce your stature.

Chapter 20:

Intentional Networking

"Although I felt prepared for the challenges of a military-to-civilian transition, the market, the psychological challenges, and the emotional toll it can have on you were a surprise. For 21 years, I knew certainty. Now, I was going into a market competing with those who never left, as well as those whom I served alongside." — Frank Clark, United States Air Force (Ret.)

While in active military service, relationships and contacts are established primarily by proximity (geography), rank, and role. There is not as much "networking" in the same sense that we network on the civilian side. I understand that one of the biggest challenges for military is that you develop networks in a vacuum. In other words, you network with the same types of people, so everyone else's networks all look the same. It is critical to start building a diverse network of contacts (military and civilian) long before you step away from the military.

Whether you are looking for a job, clients, or more interesting projects, a network will always be a critical part of your professional toolkit. In my professional career, I use intentional networking strategies to gain introductions, leads, referrals, references, insights, and relationships with stakeholders whom I deem important to my success. My intentional network is a vital part of my professional development and my circles of influence to grow my business and my career.

A network of viable contacts is critical in today's competitive business climate. Your network serves not only as lead sources for new business but also as a sounding board, support system and news source. Your network is the "circle of influence" that will guide you through your career, if carefully planned and managed.

Each of us has family, friends, and people we associate with—personally and professionally (during service and after). Your intentional network is that group of contacts you specifically recruit, maintain, and nurture to benefit from and with whom you will reciprocate. Intentional networks are win-win relationships based on rapport, trust, and mutual benefit.

Who Should be Added to Your Network?

Most people look to meet and network with decision makers—those are the hiring managers, senior leaders, and people who can transact with us. They can hire us, contract with us, and buy from us. The problem is, often they are the most sought after individuals and can get overwhelmed with inquiries.

Instead, I'd like to offer you two additional categories of contacts to consider having in your intentional network: information sources and cheerleaders. Information sources may or may not have the power to hire you, promote you, and buy from you—but they might bring some unique industry information or insight that makes you more competitive, relevant, and better at your job. For this reason, when you meet someone who is potentially a valuable information source, you network with him or her as if they are a decision maker.

Similarly, a cheerleader is a vital part of any networking strategy. These are your fans—they cheer you on when things get rough and give you support and references when you need them. Positive, supportive people are very valuable in an intentional business network.

In a Nutshell

Decision makers: Contacts who can provide you with direct leads, direct work, or bridge you to contacts who can. For example, these might be hiring managers, procurement personnel, clients, customers, and agents who can transact with and buy from you. We all need to meet decision-makers who can hire us, connect us to someone who might hire us, or refer us directly. There is no question that meeting decision-makers is valuable.

Ask Yourself:

Who are my decision makers?

_____

_____

_____

_____

Information sources: Contacts who can provide valuable insight into companies, industries, trends, and people about whom you need to know. For example, someone with a deep knowledge of marketing, human resources, or technology can be helpful as you position yourself for a new job or a promotion.

Information sources possess unique information about trends, deals, and industry insights. From personal experience, I can tell you that information sources have helped me secure new clients, attract better opportunities, and create visibility in my personal brand. They are incredibly valuable to your ability to build credibility within a market. Some of the information sources in my network have deep experience in military service, renewable energy, commercial real estate, and financial modeling. When I have a question or need insight into a company or I'm putting a proposal together for a firm that's involved in one of those sectors, I can pick up the phone and call these people. In writing this book, I have leaned on and leveraged the insights, information, and talents of many veterans who can speak to aspects of the veteran transition I couldn't possibly know. Many of your information sources will not be decision-makers in their organizations, and they may never hire you or refer you to somebody directly, but the information they can offer you—the insight and analysis that they can help with—will enabled you to win business.

Ask Yourself:

Who are my information sources?

_____

_____

Cheerleaders: Contacts who will provide references and testimonials and who will vouch for you. These contacts will give you support and encouragement. They might be a friend from your past or a colleague at your current job who is upbeat and optimistic in times of stress.

When you are networking and you meet someone who may not be a decision maker or have unique industry information but could potentially be a cheerleader, you can identify that person as a valuable contact. He or she may become a spokesperson and advocate for your brand. These people are your rock stars, your spokespeople, and your PR agents.

When you think about meeting people and intentionally designing a network that will support your professional growth, move past decision-makers and look for information sources and cheerleaders, as well. Who has valuable critical insight and information that can help you personally and professionally? Who are those cheerleaders you need to add to your database because they really make you feel good, and they'll support you and speak well about your brand?

Remember the example of Kevin at Disney (in Chapter 9)? He used his network of contacts to advocate and advance his brand in the organization. This made him an obvious choice for hire as the "expert" on all things military.

Ask Yourself:

Who are my cheerleaders?

_____

_____

_____

_____

Networking Success Tips

- As you build or enhance your network of contacts, consider that everyone you meet will potentially enter your network in one of three possible ways (decision maker, information source, or cheerleader).

- In every case, for every category of contact, certain success tips ring true. As you network, you will be engaged in a two-way dialog that must be mutually rewarding for it to work. Consider the effort, gain, and risk of each contact.

- Be sure you are mindful to:
    - **Reciprocate**. For every favor you ask (e.g., introduction to a job lead, connection on LinkedIn, or referral), be sure to return with something of greater perceived value (e.g., returned a lead, make a valuable introduction, or at least send a hand-written note of gratitude). The scales should always be tipped in your contact's favor.

- **Become a resource**. Find ways to help your contacts. Send news clippings, books, or articles of relevance. Refer a colleague to them if you think a relationship could be mutually beneficial. Be seen as a resourceful person who is connected to people and information. These are low cost ways to make a huge impact.

- **Show your authenticity**. When you are genuine, people want to get to know you and help you. If you don't know an answer to a question, say it, but then find the answer. Be that resourceful networking contact, but always show your genuine side. People connect with people.

- **Stay in touch.** Connect in person, online (on LinkedIn, for instance), and stay in touch. Even when you don't have an "ask," let your network know how you're doing, what you're up to, and what you might have to offer. Online, you might send an "Update" on LinkedIn or post on Facebook, letting your contacts know what's going on in your business or your life. Typically, we only hear from people when they need something (a job, advice, a place to stay). Be the person who stays in touch to let your network know the good things happening in your life, too.

- **Respect people's feelings**. While you might think that post was funny, it could hurt someone's feelings or damage a networking relationship. Similarly, don't share confidential or proprietary information or details unless you are 100% positive that's okay. Reciprocity means being respectful of other people's needs and feelings.

- **Respect people's boundaries.** In networking, be mindful of the limits someone is willing to go to help you. If you ask for a favor or an introduction (even when you intend to reciprocate) and the other person is hesitant or not willing, learn to be okay with that. Not everyone is comfortable sharing their database and credibility with others. Reciprocity means learning when it's okay to hear "no."

- **Become "others focused."** In networking, I recommend that you always look for the other person's favorite subject. When talking with someone new, seek out things that make them smile or laugh, rather than topics that cause their face to droop. At the holidays, many of us like to talk about college-age kids returning home or holiday traditions. Asking questions that elicit a positive response indicate you're on the right track.

Asking questions of other people, showing interest in the things that interest them, and following up with open-ended questions about their interest builds relationships. Eye contact, body language, and elevator pitches serve no good if you focus all the attention on yourself. Be sure to answer questions asked of you, but always follow up with questions to draw out the interests of the person you're speaking with.

By having a clear strategy and focus for intentional marketing and by focusing on reciprocity in building your relationships, you assume responsibility for finding and forming rewarding networking relationships. At all points in the networking process—in person and online—it is crucial to keep your reputation and vision in check. Having this clarity will allow you to act with generosity, and you will make a positive impression about your personal brand.

Base Your Networking in Authenticity

As we have been discussing, your brand strategy must be grounded in authenticity. Remember that people do business with people. Even if a company is purchasing from another company, there are human beings on both ends of the phone call. More to the point, people do business with people they like. Building rapport, ensuring the transfer of confidential information, asking favors, and reciprocating are all based on our ability to trust one another's integrity and authenticity. The more authentic we are, the less we are like that person in the room who is simply there to make contacts and meet decision-makers. The more authentic we are, the more likely we can build genuine, reciprocal relationships.

Intentional networking is a highly effective marketing strategy for your authentic personal brand.

What Networking is *Not*

Networking is not just something you do at a formal event, party, or a business reception. It's not that guy who stands in the room shaking hands and looking over you to see if somebody more important has just walked in then abandons your conversation. Networking is not just between business people who seek to generate leads. It is not just for professionals with large contact databases nor is it just for people in business development roles. As you make the transition to civilian career, you may find yourself networking in line at Starbucks, at a neighborhood barbecue, or at a job fair in your area.

Networking is about intentionally creating systematic ways you can form relationships where all the parties benefit. We all know people but how we organize that information and how we strategically leverage our personal brand to become valuable and relevant to those contacts—that's an intentional network. While we're going to have this conversation in the context of your professional growth, there is no question that a valuable intentional network will benefit you personally as well.

An intentional network requires focus, intent, and management. While your network focus is to serve your interest, which is not a bad thing, it will require giving back as much as receiving. But you will see that when we talk about an intentional network, we're not talking about the charity work that you do or the people you help in other ways. Those are philanthropic efforts that come from your heart. We are talking about a strategy that markets your personal brand.

Benefits of an Intentional Network

As we all know, our roles change over time. Our jobs change, our capacity and competency in our work change and our professional needs change. An intentional network keeps us on track through all those changes. An intentional network also provides a sounding board. Maybe you want to bounce ideas off one of your network contacts or perhaps there are some deals that you're considering. A sounding board is extremely valuable in growing your professional development.

An intentional network also provides a support system, encouragement, and referrals. I have landed jobs because of contacts in my network. I've gained client insight and won client engagements because of my network. An intentional network can provide valuable news and information. We all know that in today's market, this can give us a competitive advantage—the more information we have, the more power we have.

In a global environment, we have an expanded opportunity to market within international networks. What if you want to open an office in Beijing or Mexico City or Paris? What if you want to secure a new client in Tokyo? Having global connections and contacts around the world can be a valuable resource to you.

How to Get Started

You already have a network. The goal is to organize it and systematically tap into the results that you are looking for. As you organize your network, start listing out the people you already know. Consider: the men and women with whom you served; alumni from high school, college, grad school; colleagues and co-workers from current and past employment; people you met at events, functions, and gatherings for whom you have contact information (business phone number, email). Start putting these names into a database, such as Excel or Outlook, so you can refer to them.

Then, keep track of meetings, phone calls, notes sent, and other ways you have to contact with your network. Be sure no one gets left out. If you haven't spoken to someone in awhile, send them a handwritten note saying, "hello" with an update about your work. If you meet someone new, enter him or her into your database and begin to keep them in mind when you cross an article that might be interesting to them.

Consider:

- The people you work with

- Former colleagues from past jobs with whom you've kept in contact

- Boards of directors you sit on

- Groups, clubs, and associations that you currently belong to or even that your children participate in

- Social events that you attend

- Alumni associations (Did you go to college? How about graduate school? Do you keep in touch with any of those people?)

Also, consider cross-functional teams. Maybe you work in marketing but you really got to know the IT team in your past job. Have you kept in touch with those people? How about social connections? Maybe your kids play on the high school baseball team. How about the other people in the stands with whom you've connected? Then, of course, there is the general public you haven't even met yet.

Next, look at your potential network: Who do you need to know? In my chapter on target audiences, we talked about identifying the audiences that need to find you relevant. Who is that target audience? If there's a prospect you don't know, write that person's name down. Maybe in reading the morning's paper you identified someone you really need to get in front of and meet. Where does he work? What does he need? Does he need to know about you? (That's where your brand messaging comes in!) Write that down, too.

It will help to put this all down on paper. As you catalog your contacts (decision makers, information sources, and cheerleaders), consider developing a system that works for you. An example of how you might start organizing some of your database to reflect decision-makers, information sources, and cheerleaders is found in EXHIBIT B.

When you need a boost of encouragement or a client says, "I need to talk to some people who can vouch for you," you can then sort by your cheerleaders and get a good sense of who you can tap into. Or, if you have a specific proposal you're putting together or other projects and you need some industry insight, you can go quickly to your information sources. If you need to speak directly to prospects that may be able to hire you, you can tap into your decision-makers because you know they are people who have access to opportunity directly at their fingertips.

Exhibit B:

My Network

FIRST NAME	LAST NAME	COMPANY	PHONE	EMAIL	NOTES
Joe	Taylor	ACME Medical	000-555-1212	jtellor@host.com	Sent article on veteran hiring
Sally	Smith	ASP Aerospace	000-222-2121	sallys@host.com	Send meeting req 2/23/13
Chuck	Brown	BNN Communications	000-333-3434	cbrown@host.com	Contact Chuck after conference
Janet	Christian	WNP Asset Mngmnt	000-234-1098	janet.c@host.com	Met w/Janet 2/23/13. Send TV note
Harold	Broatman	Sky Technologies	000-235-3909	h.b@host.com	Introduce Harold to Jack Brownsbury
Manisha	Roberts	PTU Securities	000-221-7878	mroberts@host.com	Sent article on AXT security technology
Kelly	Green	Bismarck Press	000-134-0900	kgreen@host.com	Set up new meeting 2/23/13
Thomas	Taskman	MTM Diagnostics	000-989-3030	ttaskman@host.com	Contact Tom after conference
Clark	Fellows	GHT Pharmaceuticals	000-134-3934	clark@host.com	Send LinkedIn request
Robert	Blackburn	MRT Transportation	000-119-3242	rblackburn@host.com	Send TV note for meeting

190

Now that you know who you would like to connect with, consider all the sources you have identified and ask yourself, "How will I get to know them?" or "How will I get to know them better?" This is where your intentional networking strategy begins to form. This is where you start drawing concentric circles of influence: You have a network, they have a network, and their network has a network of contacts. You are looking for as many opportunities as possible for those networks to intersect.

About Them

To start forming your strategy, let's think about what you know about your current and potential contacts—your audience. Answer these questions:

- What do you know about them?

- Where do they hang out?

- What type of associations, groups, and meetings do they participate in?

- What kind of companies are they involved in?

- What are some of their hobbies? (While you might naturally think about things like golf and some of the more social hobbies, look at all possible hobbies.)

Ask yourself, "Who do they know?" Remember those concentric circles of influence around everyone you know. Who is part of their network? Who is in their circle of influence? You need to know whom they pay attention to and respect and who has credibility with them.

Where You Will Network

Once you determine this, you want to go where your prospects are. For instance, you might join the American Institute of Architects if you're an architect or the American Institute of Certified Public Accountants, if you're a CPA. Those of us in marketing might join the American Marketing Association. If you are interested in a career in human resources, consider the National Society of Human Resources Managers. If you're interested in economic development and your clients are small businesses that are looking to get funding or set roots in the community, you might find an economic development group or chamber of commerce. If you are interested in women's issues, you might seek out a women's chamber of commerce.

These groups offer you the opportunity to learn from civilians, meet other people whom you might benefit from knowing, connect with contacts at companies you otherwise couldn't meet. and more.

By all means, stay connected to your fellow soldiers and join veteran organizations. However, don't limit yourself to only joining military-related entities. You need to meet civilian employers, contacts, and networking associates. You will meet them in business and industry groups related to your new job or your search.

Finding the right industry or business groups to join takes homework. You will want to consider what the group's focus is (philanthropy? information and lead sharing? community support?) and who else is networking there as well. I have joined associations focused on mergers and acquisitions, venture capital, and financial services because many of my clients work in these sectors. Sure, some of the conversations might be a little bit over my head, but I'm there because my clients, my potential clients, and my contacts are there. I seek out my contacts rather than my peers when it comes to intentional networking. I ask myself: Where do I need to be seen? Where is my audience? Where can I learn the most?

Networking at Job Fairs

Job fairs and employment expos are typically big events where employers meet potential employees and they learn about each other. These can be great opportunities for networking. Job fairs attract hiring consultants, networking experts, marketing professionals (sometimes they work for the employers), and others with whom you could strike up a conversation. You can also learn from job seekers you meet there—what is working for them? What are they doing correctly or incorrectly? Are you setting yourself apart?

When networking at the job fair, don't arrive in uniform, unless you intend to stay in the military. Wearing a uniform sends the message that you have not made the transition. In your military training, you likely wore your one, and only, business suit to "socials." In the professional world, men wear suits and women wear dresses or suits to business events to show professionalism, appropriateness, and respect.

Your goal at a job fair or employment event is to be focused, confident, interested (and interesting), and professional.

Frank Clark, Senior Master Sergeant, USAF (Ret.), shared with me his experience transitioning from the Air Force and attending job fairs. At one in particular, he went with a focused mission: to meet the hiring manager for a company he wanted to work for.

"I ensured I had a polished resume (which is your first interview), and I networked and "gripped and grinned" with the best of them during military career fairs, civilian-sponsored job fairs, you name it," he tells me. Frank spent the day walking around the tables, meeting recruiters and shaking hands. He was prepared with a fresh stack of his well-crafted civilian resume. He carried his resumes and business cards in a leather portfolio (to avoid getting them damaged or dirty). As he was about to walk out the door, he saw a recruiter at the USAA table, which had previously been swarmed with other job seekers. "I walked up to him, shook his hand, then handed him my resume," Frank says.

The man promptly set his resume down on top of the stack he'd already accumulated. At that moment he recognized he had to make a connection, "I shook his hand again saying, 'you get hundreds of resumes a day, but not like this one.' I looked him in the eye anticipating a standard response but instead, he talked to me and asked me a few questions. The hiring manager was surprised and excited by Frank's level of confidence, knowledge of the company and it's culture, and the preparedness Frank demonstrated.

Two weeks later, a Senior Vice President needed an executive assistant for a few months. Frank had the technological and administrative skills gained in the service to support at the executive level, so he saw this as an opportunity to demonstrate the rest of his skills and abilities. In just over two years, he went from working as a temporary administrator (contractor), hired by USAA, to a Business Analyst and today Frank works as Director of Operations Support. He is also working toward a Masters Degree in Management and Organizational Leadership.

In another example, Jessie, a 20-year Navy veteran set out to pursue her dream job and found they were presenting a program and bringing hiring managers to a large job fair in her city. She did her research in advance, learned as much as she could about the company and it's hiring practices, and showed up dressed professionally and well-groomed.

When she met the hiring team at her dream company's table, Jessie was greeted with a similar response to Frank, "Just set your information over there. Here's a brochure..." Instead, Jessie took initiative. "Thank you," she calmly replied. "I can see you have a lot of interest in the open positions you're recruiting for," she continued.

"I have 15 years of experience leading teams through complex intelligence scenarios where my ability to motivate others was called upon daily. During my service in the U.S. Navy, I brought leadership with a smile and built loyalty in the teams I worked with." Her confidence and professionalism got the attention of the recruiters behind the table who were used to just collecting resumes.

Jessie continued, "I recognize your company only hires veterans who can demonstrate a willingness to serve the mission, to think outside the box, and creatively manage complex scenarios. I'm that person." Then, Jessie handed her resume and a list of testimonials she'd received which spoke to her exact skills and talents in those areas of importance to the company. "These are examples of times when I have performed to the level of excellence you hire for. I encourage you to contact my former colleagues and supervisors to learn more." This landed Jessie the interview and eventually, the job.

Networking on the Job

Once you are a part of an organization, consider joining a committee to gain visibility. Let's say you want to meet speakers and influencers in the community, the program committee of an industry association could be a great opportunity for that. If you want to meet financial executives and accountants, you might join the finance committee of a trade group.

Remember that you're looking for leadership roles and visibility in these groups you are joining. Simply attending monthly luncheon and sitting in the back of the room will rarely benefit and promote your personal brand. Joining a group or association is a part of a business strategy, so don't hang out with the same people every time you go to the monthly luncheon. Meet new people, and follow those intentional networking skills that we talked about. You're not just building your resume, you're looking to meet decision-makers, information sources, and cheerleaders who can support and encourage you as you build your brand.

There are many other ways to connect with people. How about becoming a member of hobby- and social interest related groups? Perhaps you are passionate about golf, creative writing, or dog shows. I have a very good friend who networks fabulously at dog shows. She's passionate about showing her two Beagles, and a lot of her clients have come from her networking at those events. Everyone at the dog show has something in common; it's a great place to start a conversation. You could always network within a group that's cause-related, such as veterans' rights or children's advocacy organizations, where you're going to find people who are concerned about the same issues as you are.

Other Networking

Sometimes networking comes from even more unusual places. For example, my son played on a high school baseball team. I noticed that some pretty high-powered professionals and executives whose children played on the same team often watched from the same bleachers as I did. I couldn't easily find a way to break the ice and network with them during games. But one time, the coach sent an email to all the parents and asked, "Would anybody be willing to work the snack shack this Saturday?" I looked at the list of emails, and there were some really valuable contacts in there. I could have replied just to the coach and said, "I'd be happy to work on Saturday," but instead, I hit "Reply to all" with my message. My email had my branded signature attached, as always.

I was, in fact, interrupting every other person on that email list with my message, and I considered that before sending it. But in the end, three contacts wrote me back and said, "Lida, we've sat next to each other on the bleachers for months. I didn't know you did marketing and branding —we should have a conversation." I actually secured a new client out of that email. Sometimes, you have to think creatively.

As we will talk in depth in our chapter on social networking, you also have the opportunity to connect online, and if an online strategy fits within your intentional networking strategy, there are many options to leverage. While social networking is not a replacement for in-person networking, it is a good way to share information and connect to other people.

LinkedIn, for example, removes the degrees of separation between us and multiple contacts and their circles of influence.

Facebook can connect us to childhood friends, past colleagues, fellow alumni, or people who share common personal or professional interests. Both provide multiple tools to network with people who are talking about your product or service or you.

As you develop your strategy for intentional networking, look into the online networking options that align with your personal brand, strategy, and target audience.

Where You Should NOT Network

Some places aren't appropriate for networking. I don't typically like to hang out where all my competitors are. If I'm looking for information, that's one thing, but I prefer to be where my clients are.

You also do not want to network around anything that's medical or sensitive or focused on addiction—Alcoholics Anonymous meetings, treatment centers, or grief programs, for example. These are not places where people want to have a conversation about business nor do they want to be interrupted. Many of you will have spent time in military hospitals, will attend transition assistance groups, and seek help managing effects from your war-related injuries. Conversations will naturally arise and discussions may go deep as you build relationships with fellow veterans. This is a human way to move through your grief and circumstances. To be clear, that's not what I'm suggesting under the heading of "networking."

Sometimes you shouldn't network with family and friends. Just because somebody is your neighbor doesn't mean she wants to do business with you. Just because somebody is related to you through marriage or blood doesn't mean he wants to be asked about a sensitive project. Be careful networking with people who are very close to you, either in proximity or in familial relationships.

Measure and Monitor Your Networking Efforts

How will you know if these networking efforts are working? Because you set goals and you have a strategy. You're going to measure ROI (return on investment and return on influence), because joining an association or a professional group and getting involved has to pay off. This isn't about charitable donations. We're talking about strategic marketing and promotion of a personal brand.

You will want to periodically assess whether your efforts are producing the reputation you desire and make sure that the ROI is in your favor. When I started my company, I attended any organization, networking event, luncheon, or gathering I could afford. I set a goal for myself that I would not exceed a $50 price tag. If the cost of attending a business group meeting was $30, $40, even $50, I went. My goal was to be seen and get as much information as I could. I was on a fact-finding mission to evaluate where I was going to commit my energy. If the networking events or the business forums did not include an opportunity to pass a business card or an ability to speak about what I do, it wasn't the right forum for me.

When you join, you want to get involved, so you will need to decide how much time and effort you're willing to give. In some ways it's like joining a gym: You can't just sign up and expect to lose weight. You have to commit the time and work the program to make sure you see results. What commitments are you willing to make to be involved in an association or group? You're only one person, so you're going to have to look at where your time is best spent. Make sure that you've given one hundred percent, but be sure you're getting something out of it, too. And, when you figure out which efforts are working best for you, repeat them often! One of my clients is the CEO of a successful PR agency in the Midwest. Her advice rings true for all of us: "Each day, commit fifteen minutes to promoting yourself somewhere, somehow. A small investment for a huge return!"

How to Network: Tips

As you join groups, meet new people, and expand your circle, it's very important to understand certain rules of conversation, as well as to identify the ways you can serve your network contacts. What do they need? Remember, audiences have functional needs and emotional needs. They need things tactically delivered for them, and they need emotional connections. What are they looking for? Does your audience need leads, information, or insight? Do they need to feel safe, valued, and respected? How are you best suited to help them? How can you make yourself valuable, credible, and resourceful with these contacts?

This is how the circle starts to build. With this information, you're looking for insights that will allow you to build solid, two-way relationships with people whom you've identified as valuable contacts. As you begin to meet new people, keep in mind these tips:

- **Be open to everyone.** When you go to a networking event, make it your goal to meet three new people—that's a pretty easy goal to achieve.

- **Be open-minded.** There may be a person in the room who could provide tremendous decision-making connections for you, who could be a new information source or maybe become that cheerleader you have been seeking. You won't know unless you are open to meeting all sorts of people at that event.

- **Research people before you meet them.** If you know that someone you're hoping to meet will be at a networking event, do some homework in advance. Do a LinkedIn search; Google him to see what comes up. You're looking for opportunity to build rapport, and we build rapport based on common interests.

- **Prepare some comfortable ice breakers.** You don't want to come across as a slick networker, but it couldn't hurt to have some key phrases in mind to help start a conversation. For instance, you might open a discussion with, "What brings you to today's meeting?" Somebody might answer, "Well, my boss brought me," or "I thought the program sounded interesting," which gives you a great opportunity to follow up and ask, "Well, what part of the program sounded interesting to you?"

You should be sensitive to people who might be on the brink of a not-good situation because of the economy. So you can ask the question, "How is the economy affecting your business?" That might give somebody the opportunity to say, "Wow, you know what, my business is thriving!" Great—you can have a conversation about that.

"What do you like most about your job?" is another option. Not everybody loves everything about his job, but you can get people talking about something with this query that might make them happy.

Other easy questions: Are you staying in town for the holidays? What do you do on the weekend? Do you know other people here? Always try to ask high-level, open-ended questions—not yes or no questions—to get people talking.

- **Respect boundaries.** Not everybody wants to have coffee and get to know you or introduce you to her supervisor or connect with you online. Not everybody wants to hang out with you at a networking event. Look for clues that perhaps this networking relationship isn't working out for the other person, and move away gracefully. You'll gain more credibility by doing that than you will by trying to force a relationship that isn't naturally there.

- **Don't share confidential information.** I knew a woman several years ago who was told by a very influential contact of hers that she was soon going to be interviewed for a senior sales position within the company. Someone still held the job, but as soon as it became available, she would be interviewed. The position's soon-to-be availability was highly confidential. Unfortunately, my contact, excited that she was about to be interviewed for this high-level sales position, shared that information with someone else. That person knew the person in the job—the person about to be fired.

If something like this happens to you, own your mistake as soon as possible. Go back to the person whose confidence you violated, and let her know what happened. More than likely, it's going to come back to her, anyway. You may end up losing a relationship, but you'll maintain your credibility by taking accountability and owning your mistake.

- **Don't assume that everyone recognizes your value immediately.** You may have a reputation that's taking some work to overcome. It's your job to intentionally create as much positive behavior in the direction of your desired brand as possible

- **Approach women and men.** In one of my first networking exercises with one of my veteran transition groups, several of the men in the room voiced a reluctance to approach a woman in a networking situation to initiate contact and conversation. They shared that to approach a woman, even in a business setting and even if she was surrounded by colleagues, could be perceived as "inappropriate" or "suggestive," and it made them uncomfortable.

In business, women and men co-exist in the business world. While there is still arguably disparity in pay, status, and authority, you could as easily be reporting to a supervisor who is a woman as one who is a man. The woman you might approach at a networking event could easily be a decision maker, information source, cheerleader, or other valuable contact for you in your intentional networking.

- **Clearly articulate your goals.** You want to make sure people know what you're looking for. There's an old joke about a lawyer and a banker who had golfed together for twenty-five years, when finally the banker turns to the lawyer and asks, "Over all these years, how come you've never sent me any business?" The lawyer replied, "You've never asked."

Make sure people know what you're looking for. If you're looking for a new client; if you're looking for exposure in a new market; if you're looking to be seen on stage at an industry event, be clear about how people can help you.

When I started my business, I didn't only ask people to send me clients if they knew of any who might be interested in my work, I also asked my key contacts, who were with large corporations, to help me with my exposure. I would say, "I know you often buy tables at some of these high-profile, highly influential events, and often the seat price is over my budget. If you ever have an empty seat that you're trying to fill, please call me. That's a way you can really help me."

- **Stay top-of-mind.** Meeting people is the first step, but even more important is keeping in touch with them once you've made the connection. Here's a great tip I give clients that helps them follow up after meeting somebody at an event: Before you go to that event, find a blog post or short article posted by a credible news organization. At the event, when you meet somebody and you're exchanging business cards, mention that, "You know, I just read a great article on that topic. I'm going to follow up and send it to you." Imagine his surprise and delight when he receives that as a follow-up to your conversation. Not only does it show that you're educated and informed because you offered something of value but it indicates that you follow through on promises, which is how you build integrity.

As you develop your network, keep that connection going and not just when you need something. We hear a lot from job seekers when they are out of work and then as soon as they find a job, we don't hear from them again. It's the same when people look for new business. Maybe the sales pipeline is dried up toward the end of the year and you're looking to network and fill that pipeline with work, but when you have enough work, you drop off the radar screen without contact until you need something again. This makes people feel used rather than valued.

Intentional networking needs to be worked. If you haven't talked to somebody in a while, if you haven't provided value to somebody in a while, you can't take it for granted that they will welcome you with open arms and provide you with leads or information or support.

- **Set up a routine system of keeping in contact.** Enter an item in your calendar that says, "The first Monday of every month, I will contact the first twenty people in my network database and tell them I was thinking about them and see what's going on, maybe drop them a note or an email or even a phone call. The second Monday of every month, I will go to the next twenty contacts and do the same thing." Have a system for keeping in touch with people, even if it's a monthly email that you send to everybody to let them know what you're up to.

Other ways to stay "top of mind" with networking contacts:

- **Become a resource.** When I meet with people, I get clues from our conversation about how I could be helpful to them. Often I visit people in their offices. Offices are typically decorated with things of interest to that person. The next time you're visiting with a client or contact, look around. Does your client display pictures of his family? Are there framed vacation photos of him at the beach? (If so, maybe he has an affinity for a specific location.) Did you serve in the same branch of the military? Look for cues and clues about information that you might be able to follow up with them about later.

One of my clients had artwork and photos of sailboats around his office, and I would send him articles that I came across that had to do with sailing or sailing races, and he always got a kick out of that. To him, it showed that I cared about him as a person, rather than just as a business transaction.

- **As you come across articles and invitations, forward them.** People love to get information that's relevant and valuable. No one can possibly read every article or story about their industry, and they would appreciate you staying abreast about current developments and bringing them to their attention.

I use my online social networking tools to gather information that's valuable for my clients—RSS feeds of a column in the newspaper, for example. Google and Twitter provide great tools that push information to you using keywords and search terms. If you focus on a specific area (maybe your business focuses on health care or education) and create a feed to get those articles sent to you, you can then be a resource to your contacts by forwarding that information to them.

- **Provide Introductions.** You can't introduce everyone to everybody, but if you know a great IT worker who should know a great technology director, tell them, "I'm going to make this introduction for you," and be the facilitator. It's one way to show appreciation. If somebody does something for you or has just provided valuable support or information, make sure you show your gratitude.

- **Celebrate the success of others.** Networking is about being focused on other people as well as looking out for yourself. Become a cheerleader for others who are in your network by congratulating them for their accomplishments and successes. (This also allows you to keep top-of-mind with them.)

- **Write notes.** The handwritten note is completely underestimated. Most business people appreciate the gesture of a handwritten note. I have sat with CEOs as they retrieved personalized notes from their desk drawers. Many of them recognize the time and effort someone took in sending them a personal gesture. It's beyond an email, it's beyond a typewritten note, and it is one of the most powerful tools we can use today to build relationships. Keep a stack of stamped envelopes and note cards in your portfolio, briefcase or your car. As soon as you finish a meeting, send off a personalized note of appreciation right away.

You might write:

"Thank you for taking the time to meet with me today. I enjoyed learning about your company and your vision for the next five years of growth. As you mentioned, I will follow up with you in three months to see if any positions are available at that time. In the meantime, please do not hesitate to contact me if I can be of assistance. Yours truly,"

- **Be somebody people want to be around.** When you network, you're not just looking for a job or a new client; you're looking for a relationship. Whether it's with a reporter, a prospect, a networking contact, or a fellow committee member, networking is about building relationships and showing your authenticity. Let people get to know you—the real you—and don't pretend to be someone you're not or someone you think they expect you to be.

- **Keep networking relationships balanced.** If somebody does something for you, make sure you return the favor. It doesn't have to be a lead for a lead or article for article. But if somebody helps you, make sure you help him. No one wants to enter into a networking situation where the scales are tipped, either in your favor or the other person's.

- **Know when to say "no."** Since networking is about balance, it's your job to be mindful when the scales are tipped, and somebody in your network is asking for more than she's giving. When that happens, it's time to make a change in the networking relationship.

- **Give your network time to develop.** Be patient. It's important to give your network time to grow. With intentional networking, we're not looking for one-night stands; we're looking for relationships. We're not looking for sales; we're building relationships, and that takes time. Building trust is the ultimate goal. Strive to find common ground with people, which sometimes includes small talk that's not all business.

- **Don't only hang out with other veterans.** At a business, social, or industry networking event, avoid only conversing with other veterans. While your network should include veterans (and this is the audience you likely feel safest around), force yourself to meet people who work in the industry who are not from the military side.

- **The most important thing in intentional networking is to set a game plan, a strategy.** Who do you need to know and how will you get there? It's all about sharing and collaborating. If I share an article with you and you appreciate it, send me a note. Refer somebody to me. Send me an article, or pick up the phone and tell me that you really appreciated it. It's all about give and take.

Networking can be one of your greatest assets. Consider this example: My client, Greg, had a good thing going. As a senior partner in one of the nation's largest employee benefits firms, his clients were loyal, and his appointment calendar full. New business came his way steadily. When Greg and I first met, he shared with me that his main goal was to ensure that what he was doing—and how he had been working for the past twenty-five years—was the right way going forward. He wasn't looking to fix anything that wasn't broken.

Our personal branding work brought forward the reasons behind Greg's success: His clients greatly appreciated his candor and honesty. They found him to be highly focused on their needs and not on selling. Several clients shared that Greg had built solid relationships across their companies, not just with decision-makers, showing how much he cared about each client as a company and not just as a paycheck. They shared numerous stories of how Greg offered pro-active recommendations, even when they were at a financial disincentive to him, and how he was always accessible to them and ready to answer any question. His clients viewed Greg as a true "advisor" and stakeholder in their company's future, not as a sales agent.

In creating his strategy, we didn't change any of this but simply turned up the volume, so to speak, making it easier for him to leverage his assets. For example, we developed a structured database to help Greg track, monitor, and update client information (his previous methods included "sticky notes" and writing notes on napkins), which allowed him to remember birthdays, special occasions, and other important dates more efficiently. We structured his in-person networking to be more focused and intentional, rather than casual and by happenstance so he could leave less to chance than before. We also created a tracking system so he could follow up and monitor the effects of his networking. We then set him up with an account for an electronic communications tool so he could regularly schedule e-newsletters and announcements to his client database. This tool also allowed him to stay top-of-mind with prospects, promoting his "high touch" and approachable value proposition.

These tactics and the overarching strategy were manageable and fun for Greg, and they took hold immediately. Within weeks, his clients began forwarding his communications to prospects he should meet, and he received very positive feedback from prospects that appreciated his attention to relationships, not just a sale. For Greg, personal branding revealed the many things he was doing right, so he could confidently and effectively continue to market himself in ways that felt authentic and produced great results.

Asking for Recommendations From Your Network

An important part of being perceived as credible (particularly as you interview for a job) and building your personal brand is creating a narrative for how you want to be known and making sure others understand that narrative. You want to be sure that when someone introduces or refers you, they are able to highlight the specific values, qualities, skills, and attributes you want to be known for. As I've written about many times before, you can't be positioned as an "expert" in everything. You have to be specific. As you transition into a civilian career, it is important to work on that narrative when you ask for recommendations, introductions, referrals, or testimonials.

Whether you are asking for recommendations online or in person, here are some things to remember:

- **Make it easy for the person giving you the recommendation.** When you ask for a recommendation, offer to provide clear talking points for them to address. This is particularly important as you translate your military resume and experience into civilian terms.

Specify the key words for them to use (e.g., for a job in information technology project management, you can ask the recommender to use the phrase "IT specialist" and "IT project management" instead of "technology guru" to help your chances for the job).

- **Consider the format.** On social networking sites like LinkedIn, for instance, recommendations can only be provided by someone with a LinkedIn profile. Be sure you ask colleagues or supervisors who are able to give recommendations (some companies prohibit recommendations and endorsements as company policy). You will have the opportunity to review the recommendation and offer changes to a it before it is posted on your LinkedIn account.

- **Provide guidance and suggestions.** When someone offers you a written or phone recommendation, it is possible to be more descriptive and detailed. For this reason, you want to give your recommender as much guidance as possible. Translate your military terminology and jargon into a language that civilian hiring managers will understand. Again, your key points and desired positioning will be important. Don't go overboard with pages of notes and suggestions for the recommender, but it will be appreciated if you can outline the talking points you'd like highlighted.

- **Consider the source.** Asking former coworkers and service men/ women to give recommendations may carry different weight and importance than if you ask your former or current supervisor or even the president/CEO of the company. Consider which person would be seen as more credible and influential to the recipient of the recommendation. That said, remember that certain companies and professionals do not allow recommendations as they can be seen as endorsements (and can bring legal and human resources implications).

- **Consider other sources.** You might also consider recommendations and testimonials from community members, professionals you have collaborated with on projects, and people you know in business who can vouch for your skills, character, work ethic, and talents.

- **Be prepared for them to say "no".** Just because you ask for a recommendation or testimonial does not mean the person is comfortable offering one. They might not feel that they have had enough experience with you, or maybe they have not been too happy with your work (and didn't tell you). Or, as mentioned above, they may not be able to offer you one because of company policy. When someone recommends you on a public platform, like LinkedIn, it shows on their profile as well, and that might make some people uncomfortable.

- **Say thank you!** Be sure to follow up with a handwritten note for a recommendation or testimonial. The person who offered to vouch for you took the time and made the effort, and it should be recognized. They also leveraged their own credibility to support you. Be sure to keep them posted on the opportunity you were recommended for, particularly if it was a job or client opportunity.

Offering recommendations are a wonderful way to celebrate people you've served or worked with, sharing their talents with others. Be mindful of those recommendations you give because you are leveraging your own reputation in vouching for others. And, reputation is everything!

Ask Yourself:

What is my objective in networking?

_____

_____

_____

_____

Who do I know (list everyone in your target company or industry)?

_____

_____

_____

_____

Who do I need to know?

_____

_____

_____

_____

Who can connect me to those contacts?

_____

_____

_____

_____

How will I approach those contacts?

_____

_____

_____

_____

_____

Key Takeaways:

- Intentional networking is a way to systematically develop a network of contacts that benefit you, who have your best interest at heart, and with whom you can reciprocate through a system and a strategy.

- When networking, be a resource. You want people to rely on you. Look for opportunities to share information, collaborate, refer, and offer something of value.

- Keep in contact. Networking is about relationships, and it requires keeping in touch more often than just when you need something.

- Respect people's boundaries. If a person seems uncomfortable with your request or unwilling to help you, recognize that you may be crossing a professional line or bumping up against her boundary for how far she is willing to go to help you.

- Reciprocate often. Whether your networking contacts are information sources, cheerleaders, or decision-makers, don't forget the balance of give and take. It's not all about you.

- Follow up. If somebody has helped you, let him know how it turned out. Did you actually form an engagement with the person he referred you to? What did you learn?

- Remember to thank others. If somebody has really done something special for you, write a handwritten note or pick up the phone and let her know how much it meant to you.

Chapter 21:

Your Visual Brand Identity

In this chapter, we will dive into your visual personal brand identity: how you crisply and effectively present visually what you do and what makes you stand out. Here you will learn how to position yourself with a look, feel, and tone to the audience that needs to find you relevant.

Your Personal Marketing Impression

As someone new to the civilian career market, you are trying to stand out in a sea of similarity. While you might feel you are competing against civilians workers for each opportunity, you are also competing against recent college grads and fellow veterans. The advent of desktop publishing, affordable online design tools, and inexpensive marketing materials means everyone tries to outdo each other when it comes to visual marketing and collateral. If you don't begin with a strategy based on your personal brand (and authentic passions, talents, and goals,) you run the risk of blending in, looking like everyone else and missing the opportunities you desire.

217

Your personal brand comes to life through the impression you make, from the way you dress to the words you say to the business card you hand me in our first meeting. Let's say I was presenting a workshop at your company and you were told that you were going to see a presentation from an expert in the field of brand development, someone who has represented leading executives, companies, and organizations around the world in owning and managing their reputations. Then you witnessed a messy, uninspiring presentation, and collected a boring business card from me. Would my brand impression confirm or dispel my positive reputation?

In personal branding, we can spend time and money developing our message and value proposition, defining our talents and passions, and targeting our audiences. Yet it can all fall apart when it comes to presenting our brand through our marketing image. Many people have fallen into this trap in the reverse. They design snazzy websites, clever business cards, and cutting-edge YouTube videos, yet when you meet them, there is nothing snazzy or inspiring about them. Their marketing impression does not match who they are authentically. It appears they just found some clever designers or online tools.

Your marketing materials should reflect your brand. Your colors, logo (if you get one), style, and image should be examined in a broader context. They need to be evaluated from the standpoint of whether they support your personal brand, attract and appeal to your target audience, and reinforce your value to that audience.

Example:

When I first met Sandy, she was hesitant to talk about "all this branding stuff" because what she needed instead, she said, was a corporate identity package for her new business. She had left her post as corporate counsel for one of the largest consumer goods manufacturers in the U.S. and was beginning a consulting business around corporate communications. She wanted marketing pieces, not messaging.

But when I shared the value of creating the messaging first, Sandy understood that her marketing pieces and collateral would have greater meaning and impact if we focused on her vision and passion before looking at fonts and colors.

Going through the personal branding process—identifying her values, competitive advantage, and target audiences—clarified several things for Sandy. First, she began to articulate why she didn't like working in some companies and with certain types of clients and why other companies and clients made her enjoy her work and want to give more. She realized, for example, that she truly enjoyed working in male-dominated industries where her voice would be unique, rather than typical. She enjoyed being "special" and different. She also realized she wanted to work with clients who were focused on action, not just talk. Clients she had worked with who enjoyed long process and slow movement frustrated her. Her sweet spot was with companies that needed solutions quickly and were prone to act swiftly.

In this way, she was able to pinpoint the specific programs she felt most passionate about offering. These were the ones that attracted the most attention and gave her the most reward, personally and financially.

When it came time to design and develop a complete corporate identity package for Sandy's business, from logo to website, we based everything on her passions, values, vision, and target audience. As we hit each sample and proof, we'd ask, "Does this look and feel like the Sandy you want others to see?" Giving Sandy the filter and the power to make intentional decisions freed her to successfully launch her business and never look back.

I encourage you to reflect on your brand promise and your desired brand, as well as your intended audience. These are the foundational elements of your strategy from which you can craft the look and feel of your brand. I also encourage you to think of your superhero moment. How did you show up then? When are you feeling your most confident and empowered? What look, image, and colors fuel that feeling for you?

Would You Find *You* Interesting?

From business cards to websites to resumes, we all use tools to market ourselves. If you work for a large company, you won't have as much opportunity to customize your marketing materials as a representative of the organization. But if you own your business, promote yourself independently, or are in a job search, you have an opportunity to customize the way that you market yourself.

As you think about your visual branding, consider this question: would you be attracted to you, based on how you market yourself?

You're trying to attract people—your target audience—who will find you relevant, whose values and interests likely align well with yours. So, would you find you interesting, and how does that show up in your marketing?

Whenever I prepare a brand framework for a corporate, non-profit, or executive client, we focus the marketing and communications strategy on tone and positioning. Your tone reflects the attitude of your marketing and how you communicate what's important to you and what you believe in. Your tone provides a filter, a set of criteria through which you'll determine, "Is this the right feel and attitude for my marketing?" All this is rooted in authenticity, but the tone really gives us a differentiator. It helps you decide if your communication is upbeat and friendly or serious and sophisticated. What is the tone you want your marketing to project?

Example:

If you are seeking to be positioned as a well-read and worldly leader, able to motivate teams of analysts in the financial services industry, you might create a marketing tone that is confident, scholarly, and approachable.

Your positioning reflects the company that you keep and the way that you are received. In other words, what will you be known for? Who will you be seen with, interact with, and strengthen relationships through? How will you position your value to your target market based on the emotional brand benefits you want them to receive from you? What is the positioning that you're looking to achieve?

Using my example above, you might be positioning yourself as professional, capable, and interested in others. After all, it takes a strong and capable leader to be able to learn about the people who report to him.

Furthermore, you might consider your tone and positioning, for example, to be traditional, classic, and timeless. You might think about brands that adopt this positioning, such as Tiffany, Crane's Stationery, or Brooks Brothers. They don't show a lot of flair; there isn't a lot of going outside the box. They reflect a pretty traditional, timeless, classic, maybe even conservative type of tone and posturing. Their target audiences know they produce quality products for which customers will spend a bit more money. Their audiences rely on a level of consistency and the emotional benefits that come with status, elegance, and timeless quality.

Or perhaps you see yourself as professional but with a slight edge. You might project a polished, clean, professional image but with a little spin. Perhaps that spin is humor or something that's a bit unexpected. Brands like Ralph Lauren do a great job here, or Dove soap, a conservative, expected brand that uses a little bit of humor, fun, and edge in its marketing.

You might instead consider your brand to be about making a creative impact. If you're in an artistic field—a designer, a photographer, an advertising executive—you likely want to make a creative impact. You might relate to a brand like Apple computer or other companies that target creative audiences.

If you were to assign yourself to one of these three categories of tone and positioning examples, which do you see yourself aligning with best?

Traditional/classic/timeless? Professional but with an edge? Creative, with impact?

Let's say you identify with the traditional, conservative look. You might produce business cards that look a bit more expected. They would likely be very clean, crisp, upfront, and with nothing unexpected to throw your audience off. The style can be a little bit bold but still offer that professional, conservative look. These are completely acceptable, very well received marketing pieces that support the traditional, conservative look, and will give comfort to your target audiences, who are likely looking for that level of reassurance from the professionals they hire.

Perhaps you consider yourself a little bit more on the professional-with-an-edge scope? When I created my LIDA360 marketing tools, I considered whether I wanted to be seen as traditional and conservative or someone looking to make a creative impact with my audiences. Those of you who are familiar with the LIDA360 brand will know that I chose the middle. My colors, tone, website, the images I use to illustrate and communicate—everything has a little bit of an edge to it. I chose bold, energetic, vibrant colors and images but retained a professional posturing and positioning for my work. All this was intentionally designed and is intentionally integrated into all my marketing materials, from my website to my business cards to my presentation templates.

If, like me, you consider yourself a little bit more in the professional-with-an-edge category, you might look at designs that incorporate some fun or whimsy. They will still appear clean and crisp but a bit more playful. Your marketing should be consistent with your brand image and tone to ensure it's received well by your target audiences.

Now let's say you choose to make a creative impact. You might consider marketing materials that are unconventional and have an element of surprise to them. Have you ever seen a metal business card? How about a translucent brochure? Maybe your website is an interactive flash demo of your product? If it's important to you to be seen as clever or funny or to stand out in a way that demonstrates your creative craft, you might design a brochure that wraps around pieces of bubblegum like a comic strip. The possibilities are endless; let your creativity be your guide.

The point of this exercise is that you want to make sure you stand out from your competitors, manage how you are perceived, and back up the look of your marketing with your personal presence and actions.

As you articulate your value, tone, and positioning and begin to develop a "look" for your marketing materials, consider each piece you craft as an extension of that feeling, a reflection of the desired brand you want your target audience to experience. Each piece you create, from your business card to your website to your email signature, should reinforce the value proposition you are putting forward.

Creating a Lasting Marketing Impression

While you're considering your marketing identity, also ask yourself, "Will this look have a shelf life? Will it have longevity?" If you tap into popular trends for your brand identity, you may run the risk of having to redo your branding in six months or two years. That can be confusing for your audience and expensive for you. Consider something that you can live with for a while and that you'll be proud to hand out as a reflection of you. Choose an image that allows you to show confidence and creativity and all the posturing traits that you set up for yourself but that is going to have some shelf life.

Business Cards

Even in today's digital world, there is a need and value to the printed business card. Imagine you meet a great contact or prospect at a business networking event or even at a coffee shop. What are the odds that you will have a copy of your resume with you or would be likely to hand it over? A business card is similar to a "calling card" when you are unemployed. You will create one that represents your personal brand, clearly shows how you can be reached (phone, email, regular mail), and may even include a few keywords or a tagline as a descriptor for your specialty or targeted industry.

Guidelines for your first personal business card:

- Print on quality paper. This does not have to be costly. There are many stationary and office supply stores, as well as online services, who print high quality business cards for little cost. You will want to avoid the business cards that you print at home since the perforations and smudges are typically giveaway signs that you tried to save money.

- Don't go super fancy. Avoid high gloss paper stock, bold images (unless they are specific and very important to your industry), cartoons, and fancy fonts (typestyle). Simple and elegant is preferred over distracting and busy.

- Consider listing your cell phone number instead of your home phone. If you have a family, the risk is that a child could answer the phone and hurt your first impression with a new business contact. Your cell phone will also have a voicemail unique to you, which you also control and can listen to in private.

- Be careful about the email address you use professionally. I see many email addresses from veterans that read: GIJoe2GetYou@Host.com or BigGuns4Hire@Host.com. This is not professional and sends the message that you are still in active duty. Instead, use your first name, middle initial (if you use it), and last name. If that name is taken, consider adding a simple number or punctuation. For example. ThomasJHoward@Host.com or Thomas.Howard@Host.com or ThomasHoward223@Host.com.

- If you have spent time and resources building your LinkedIn profile, consider adding it to your business card. Similarly, if you have an online profile or resume posted, you can also add that link.

Consider leaving the back blank (so you or the recipient can write a note) or add a statement that speaks to your career passions. Here are some samples of business cards are found in EXHIBIT C:

EXHIBIT C:

Ask Yourself:

How do I want to be perceived?

_____

_____

_____

_____

How should my marketing materials look?

_____

_____

_____

_____

Do I have a tagline? Is it relevant to my career transition?

_____

_____

_____

_____

Do I need marketing materials other than a business card?

_____

_____

_____

_____

Key Takeaways:

- Your marketing materials should support your personal brand, appeal to your target audience, and reinforce your value to that audience.

- Branding is about making a connection that is consistently reinforced. As you develop a visual marketing identity for your personal brand, focus on being integrated and consistent across your materials, language, and look.

- Take into account the interests of your target audience. Would you find _you_ interesting and compelling? Create marketing pieces that would get your attention.

- Strive for a tone in your marketing materials that feels authentic to you. Are you projecting an attitude of confidence, safety, and approachability? Or, are you creating a tone of exclusivity and aloofness? Either way, the tone of your personal brand must come through in your marketing to be effective, and it must feel comfortable to you.

- Develop marketing materials that have a long shelf life. Unless you plan to update your materials often and have a strategy for reintroducing them to your audience, look for identity materials that reflect your passion and genuineness, not the trends that are fashionable today.

Chapter 22:

Personal Style, Wardrobe, and Image

If you wore a uniform your entire military career, you may be asking, "How do I dress appropriately for a job on the civilian side?"

One of the first realities I encountered when I began working with transitioning military veterans was the lack of information available to help you with understanding style, wardrobe, and image norms in the civilian sector. I remember in my first class in Philadelphia, a brilliant and decorated officer stopped me mid-sentence as I talked about wearing a suit to a job interview. He asked, "When you say 'a suit,' is that where the jacket and the pants match?" He followed up by explaining, "I've worn green and blue for 25 years. Please explain so I can understand."

Those of us who stayed in the civilian sector have grown up reading style magazines, watching the career advice television shows, and are familiar with the trends in fashion. In this chapter, we'll focus on your personal style and image because the way you present yourself says a lot about who you are, what you value, and what others can expect in a relationship with you.

Your style and image should be appropriate to the situation, the people present, and the work you'll be performing. There is no one-size-fits-all "uniform" for the professional environment on the civilian side.

Since I am a personal branding specialist, I focus my clients on how they want to be perceived and the reputation they want to earn. Your personal brand comes to life in how you consistently behave, promote, and present yourself (image) to others. In all of my writing and speaking, I share many of the ways you can uncover your personal brand assets, create a strategy for promoting and positioning yourself, and be intentional in how you show up (image, body language, tonality, etc.)

The Importance of the First Impression

Have you ever heard, "You have one chance to make a good first impression"? We form judgement quickly based on what someone looks like, how they sound, how they act, and what they actually articulate. Researchers have looked into the question of exactly how much of our body language, vocal tonality, and expressions create the message received and how much is the actual information communicated. In Albert Mehrabian's studies in the late 1960's he drew conclusions that indicate the value of non-verbal communication impacting messages received to be possibly as high as almost 90%![11] This indicates that how you say something and how you sound could be almost more important that what you actually say.

---

[11] http://en.wikipedia.org/wiki/Albert_Mehrabian

Others have questioned the percentages[12], but the impact remains clear: what you say must be matched consistently with how you say it to drive impact.

In the first five seconds after meeting you, someone has judged you, possibly as credible, confident, and professional or as interesting, valuable, and trustworthy or as lazy, disorganized, and insecure.

A 2009 New York University study revealed that not only will people judge us quickly based on superficial qualities, but they will determine whether they like us in that initial judgment as well.[13]

If I perceive you to be arrogant and unapproachable, I'm less likely to want to get to know you and learn what you do and need. You miss an opportunity to have me help you meet your goals. Perception and judgment aren't fair. But other people's perception of us is their reality, and they will give us opportunity, assign us value, and create visibility for us based on what they believe to be real.

First impressions are subconscious and judgmental. Your goal in a personal branding journey is to help other people form positive judgments about you, offer you opportunities to grow and succeed, and see your genuineness and passion. If your first impression leaves an undesirable taste in their mouths, you will be quickly discounted instead.

---

[12] http://www.psychologytoday.com/blog/beyond-words/201109/is-nonverbal-communication-numbers-game

[13] http://www.nyu.edu/about/news-publications/news/2009/03/08/scientists_identify_the_neural.html

Ask Yourself:

What first impression do I make?

_____

_____

_____

_____

Start With Your Goals

To have maximum impact over your first impression, as well as your lasting impression, set a goal for how you want others to perceive you. Think about words like confident, capable, friendly, stylish, and polished. Then, evaluate whether you are sending the right message with the way you are dressed and present yourself. Does your clothing look outdated while your goal is to be seen as contemporary and polished? Does your wardrobe make you look old, while you are trying to network with a younger audience? Are your clothes oversized and sloppy, making you appear disheveled and unorganized?

Image and style are ways we package ourselves to attract other people. When our image is appropriate, we are able to build relationships and can advance towards our goals. When our image is inconsistent with our values or is inappropriate to the situation, we can repel people who hold value to us.

When shopping for your civilian work wardrobe, choose clothes that are appropriate for your body (size and shape) and your job. Always buy the best quality you can afford. Look for sales and promotions at various local stores, at your mall, or at online retailers. Variety is not as important as quality. Invest in the basics and grow your wardrobe from there.

Grooming Counts!

We often focus so much on our clothing and wardrobe that we forget one of the most important elements of an effective image: grooming. Personal grooming is not typically an issue with recently separated veterans. However, I have known many who are so excited about experimenting with hair length, facial hair, and other grooming areas that they veer too far in the other direction (from the conservative military requirements). One Army veteran shared with me, "After leaving service, a lot of men enjoy the freedom to grow a beard, mustache, or goatee because they don't have to shave every day."

When I was a department hiring manager in the financial services industry, I immediately noticed when a candidate had dirty fingernails, unkempt hair, wasn't freshly shaved, or had a button missing from his jacket.

While your appearance, image, and style won't land you a job, it certainly can hurt you getting the job you want. Make sure you present yourself in a way that's consistent with your values and interests and is appropriate to the situation.

How to Best Present Yourself

Consider the impression you think your personal style should set with other people. How do you think people perceive you when you walk into the room? Do they see you as someone who is confident, strong, and high-energy or maybe they judge you as shy, reserved, and insecure.

Write down some notes around the perception you'd like your image to create. How would you like people to see you? Would you like to be seen as friendly, approachable, and confident? How about bold, expressive, and creative?

Ask Yourself:

What impression would I like to make on others when they first meet me?

_____

_____

_____

_____

Next, consider your target audience. How do they dress? How do they typically dress? Are they usually dressed conservatively and professionally? Write down some notes about how your audience presents itself.

Ask Yourself:

How does my target audience dress?

_____

_____

_____

_____

Looking at both sets of your answers, do they align? Do you dress in a way that creates your desired image? And does that image work with what your audience expects?

I remember a lunch with a new client who positions herself as an innovative leader in the field of organizational development and leadership training. She targets high-technology clients who are at the inflection point of tremendous growth. Her marketing materials are slick, very cutting edge. Her website has more bells and whistles than an amusement park ride! Yet, upon meeting her, I was struck by her appearance and style. Her clothes were outdated and ill-fitting. Her haircut was befitting someone much older and more serious. Her style was not that of someone hip and cutting edge.

In working together, we addressed the disconnection between how she marketed herself—from her website to the language on her LinkedIn profile to her marketing materials—and how she presented herself in person. Which was the real her? Bringing her image into alignment with her marketing approach and her clients' needs created the credibility she sought and removed the distraction of the disconnection.

Flair and self-expression can reveal themselves in many appropriate ways, depending on your goals and objectives. Sometimes, you want to set yourself apart from your competitors. If you have the personal presence to pull it off, you can get away with something bold. I know of an attorney on the East Coast who is known for wearing orange Converse tennis shoes. He wears them with a suit. He wears them to court. He wears them to depositions and to client meetings. This isn't a hit-and-miss thing—he's known for these orange Converse tennis shoes. There's even an orange tennis shoe illustration on his business card. It's part of who he is; it's part of his style and very much reflects the way he handles himself in court and with clients. It is something that he's known for and is part of his brand.

Building Your Wardrobe

As you have the resources, build pieces into your wardrobe that allow you to mix and match when you need to. You always want your style to reflect who you are and where you are. East Coast styles tend to be dressier, West Coast typically more relaxed. Financial services industry is more conservative and artistic agencies are more laid back. Whatever environment you're in, your style should not distract or cause your credibility to be questioned. Your style should enhance your personal brand!

Here I will lay out some of the basics, assuming you are newly transitioned and haven't spent a great deal of time (or money) on a professional wardrobe.

The Suit

Traditionally, suits are matching jackets and pants/skirts of the same fabric pattern, weight, and style. Modern suits may be "athletic" cut, slim fitting, or "robust" sized. Most every retail store has their own type of signature suit that they market to consumers.

As you look for your first suit, consider where and how you'll be working. Will you be in an office all day? Will you be meeting with clients? Will you be walking outdoors or hopping into taxis regularly? How formal will your clients be dressed?

As I've mentioned before, buy the best quality you can afford. Always try a suit on and go for the most classic fit, fabric, and style possible. Trends and fashion change often, and you might limit the longevity of your purchase by going with something hip and trendy. Instead, wait until your wardrobe is built up before you invest in more fashion-forward pieces.

Some men's suits are year round wool fabrics that hold up very well. Regular cleaning and care is needed to ensure the suit holds its shape, and men can accessorize and modify the look of the suit by changing the necktie, adding shirts such as french-cuff with cufflinks, and tie stays. A good quality suit should last you several years.

Women can be feminine or formal in a suit. Oftentimes, we change up the blouse and accessories to change the tone and look of a suit. A solid color suit will give women the most flexibility to add accessories, shoes, blouses/camisoles and belts to transform the suit to a new look.

238

Dress Shirts

Today, men's dress shirts come in a myriad of colors, patterns, and fits. From pink to white to checked to paisley; from monogramed cuffs to french cuffed; from athletic cut to hefty shape, men have a lot of options! My advice is the same—start with the basics and build from there. Every man's wardrobe should contain one good quality white dress shirt. This can be paired with a suit and tie or with dress slacks or Khakis for a more casual look. Dark skinned men tend to look best in pale colors, as do men with darker features (hair and eyes). Be careful if you are fair skinned and have light hair—too white of a shirt can wash you out. Perhaps look for one that leans more ivory, than pure white. Good advice is to purchase your dress shirts and ties (if you can) at the same time you purchase suits to be sure they all work together. Personal shoppers and store clerks in men's stores are often well trained to advise on color combinations and patterns. Your goal is to ensure the look is consistent with your authentic personal brand and appropriate for the industry and company you are pursuing.

Separates

Many business environments today permit something called "business casual" which means you don't have to wear a suit or professional attire to the office or on the job. In this case, you can mix and match slacks, jackets, skirts, and blazers along with sweaters, blouses, and shoes to create a more casual but still professional look. Each company (and geography and industry) seems to define business casual dress differently. Follow the appropriate guidelines of the company you work for.

Separates are a great way to extend your business wardrobe. For men, having one or two pairs of nice dress slacks along with Khaki or Dockers-type pants work well. Wear them with sports shirts (short or long sleeve) and a belt/shoe combination that reflects your job and company. Sports shirts are shirts that are not designed to be worn with a tie. They typically have a bold pattern, pocket on the breast, and don't require a jacket on top. In some cases, "polo" type shirts can be used as a sports shirt, but this is a more casual option.

If you opt to wear a jacket or sports coat, consider the event or situation and the other items you will be wearing. According to Wikipedia, a sports coat is defined as,

> A sport coat, sport jacket, also called a sports coat or sports jacket, less commonly sport coat, is a jacket for men. Though it is of a similar cut and length to a suit jacket, there are several differences. First, a sport may be worn on less formal occasions than a suit would be. Also, it is designed to be worn on its own, without matching trousers, and does not come as part of a suit. Styles, fabrics, colors and patterns are also more varied than in most suits; sturdier and thicker fabrics may be used, such as corduroy, suede, denim, leather and tweed.[14]

For business casual, some companies permit tennis shoes and sandals. To be on the safe side, wear boat/deck shoes (e.g., Sperry Top-Sider shoes)

---

[14] http://en.wikipedia.org/wiki/Sports_coat

or slip-on leather shoes. Always watch what others do first. If you are encouraged to dress comfortably and more casually, be sure your clothes are clean, free from tears or wear, and don't display any offensive slogans, logos, or marks. The workplace is not the forum for political expression through clothing.

Women can take advantage of a more lenient wardrobe when it comes to mixing separates. Skirts (long, short, full, A-line), pants (flared, wide-legged, tapered, capri), tops (blouses, sweaters, etc.), and shoes come in overwhelming choice for many women. Again, look around to see what others wear at that company or office, and be sure your style is not creating a distraction.

Shoes

Men: Many style experts suggest men match their belts and shoes to create a uniformed look for a suit or even separates. Men's dress shoes come in many styles and types. From the traditional wingtip or classic lace up, the options for a man's dress shoe range widely. When in doubt for the best shoe to start with, consult with an expert in your local shoe store who can consider the suit or slacks you will wear the shoes with. To begin, stick with the classic colors: black, brown, or tan to compliment the most looks.

For women, shoes that are an appropriate height to walk in comfortably and elongate the calf will present well. If you are not used to wearing dress shoes then practice outside and inside before wearing them to an interview or important meeting. A classic pump or heel will compliment most dresses, skirts/blouses/blazers, and suits (even pants). Sandals and ultra high heels should be worn sparingly in most professional environments.

Women building a professional wardrobe should start with shoes in neutral, classic colors: black, nude, navy, and brown. As you accumulate pieces, consider adding different colors, patterns, and textures.

Socks

Many military personnel have not had to decide which socks to wear, as uniforms are defined for them. That said, socks can be subdued and traditional (color should coordinate with your slacks) or can actually be a perfect place for men to add some flair to their wardrobe. I know a senior business executive in a very conservative company who travels frequently. He is required to wear a traditional suit for work. His personality is lively, fun, and outgoing. The place he expresses that side of himself is through his socks. When people meet him for the first time, they are often entertained and delighted by his choice of socks that day, and clients who know his flair always anticipate his sock choice when they see him.

Necktie

Another place men can really express personality and power is in the necktie. A strong red tie conveys strength and authority, while a pastel tie full of cartoon characters shows whimsy and playfulness.

Men should pay attention to the tie as much as the suit. When you wear a tie, consider the statement the tie makes (or doesn't), and make sure it matches the rest of the look. Mixing patterns is acceptable in menswear, but refer to an expert in a retail store or read about trends and fashion in magazines to get advice. This is not an area where you can make it up as you go along and it always works out. Especially if you are in a conservative business (e.g., finance, law, government), appropriateness is critical.

Dresses

More and more women seem to be comfortable in dresses these days. From full length to wide bottom to short and tailored, dresses seem to be making a business comeback. Women can wear dresses of varying fabric and pattern, noting that many dresses work well with sweaters and blazers, too. In the winter, women can wear tights and boots with dresses and in the summer, pumps or sandals can be appropriate for the office.

Jewelry and Eyeglasses

As with all wardrobe pieces, the goal is not to distract or offend with jewelry. Body piercings, overly religious jewelry, or "noisy" pieces (that clink together as you talk or move) are distracting in most business environments. Jewelry (for men and women) can be a way to self-express and change the look of a wardrobe and should be used to enhance your look, not take away from it.

If your personality is such that you want to express yourself visually in a bold way, why not consider a pair of statement eyeglasses? This can be an easy way to build a memorable brand consistent with your personality. I've known several creative people who've dressed conservatively, yet paired a bold pair of eyeglasses to show their personality at work. Consistency is important. If you want your eyeglasses to be a part of your look, you need to wear them often.

Ways to Illuminate Your Personal Style

Your goal is always to be recognized for your uniqueness, but not everyone would be able to wear orange Converse sneakers and get away with it. Being unique doesn't mean wearing a clown suit when everyone else is in a business suit.

Your target audience wants you to be comfortable. In expressing your personal brand, particularly in a business setting, the goal is to show consistency with your personality, passion, and interest and still be appropriate for the occasion.

Do's and Don'ts for Building a Personal Style

Do:

- Always dress one notch above your target audience. If your audience wears slacks and sweaters, try a light blazer on top. If your audience wears jeans and T-shirts, make sure yours are pressed and high quality.

- Be yourself. Have you ever put on a jacket that a store clerk insisted you take home, but you don't love it? I have, and the whole time I'm wearing it I feel like I'm not being myself. On the other hand, I have put on outfits that make me feel like a rock star. I love to wear things that make me feel happy, confident, and comfortable. Then I'm more able to be myself and engage with other people. When I'm distracted by something that someone else chose for me, something that doesn't feel right; it feels like a costume to me, and I'm sure my audience can sense that.

- Choose a wardrobe that's appropriate for your age and body shape. Appropriateness means that you dress age appropriately and wear clothing that fits you and is not distracting in a negative way.

- Update your style periodically. You can do this by hiring a professional stylist, reading magazines and books, getting help online, or seeking counsel from someone you trust. If your wardrobe starts to feel tired and boring to you, it likely isn't making a great impression on other people.

- Spend money on quality pieces. Buy the best you can afford and build a wardrobe over time. Start with the investment pieces and grow the accessories as you can afford them.

- Make friends with a tailor. A small investment in tailoring could make a huge difference in how you look.

- Consider how others will feel about your dress. Could your wardrobe offend some people? Is the image you project creating a positive impression?

- Pay attention to your grooming. More often than not, hair that is neat, trimmed, and clean, along with facial hair that is trimmed and hands that are well-groomed will make a positive impression.

Don't:

- Forget to make sure your clothes are pressed and clean.

- Neglect your shoes: always polish your shoes and check the soles for holes and stickers.

- Share your love of self-marking too early. It's always safest to cover visible tattoos; remove piercings (except ears, for women), and avoid jewelry that is too revealing about your love of alternative music.

- Forget to check your breath! A good first impression can be crushed by a toxic plume of bad breath. Keep mouth freshener in the car or in your bag before going into an interview or job situation.

- Try to be somebody else. Find your own style and embrace it!

- Miss an opportunity to relay the benefits of your brand. If you're an outgoing, approachable, confident person, make sure that shines through your image, and don't lose sight of your strategy. This is all about a plan, and it's about intentionally creating the reputation that you seek in the marketplace.

Ask Yourself:

What is the environment of the job I am pursuing? Casual? Formal?

_____

_____

_____

_____

What is a comfortable style for me?

_____

_____

_____

_____

What is my wardrobe budget?

_____

_____

_____

_____

What wardrobe pieces do I need to buy first?

_____

_____

_____

_____

Key Takeaways:

- Style says a lot about who you are, what you value, and what others can expect in a relationship with you. Think about whether you are sending the right message and creating the most powerful first impression that you can with your personal appearance.

- Strive for consistency. Create a look for yourself that is comfortable and reflects your true inner style. If you like color, embrace it. If you prefer muted tones, that's great. Whatever tone and style you choose, look for that style to reflect who you are across all of your appearance, from your grooming to your wardrobe to your complete presence.

- Be yourself in the way that you dress. How you present yourself influences your emotional state and your attitude. If you are comfortable about the way you look, your sincere, authentic personality is more likely to shine through.

Chapter 23:

Body Language

As many of you learned during your military training, the power of body language to communicate is not to be overlooked. During combat, you learned how to interpret and understand the nuances of threat/opportunity based on whether there was a match between words and body language subtleties. You learned that the slightest move could trigger a series of reactions. In combat, the unintended circumstances from subconscious body language can be costly—even deadly. On the civilian side, it is more likely that someone will misunderstand or misjudge you, positively or negatively.

Your personal brand comes to life through the way that you present yourself and behave. Your body language expresses your confidence level, mental state, and emotions. It reflects whether you're scared, happy, frustrated, or angry and whether you can be trusted.

You may recall our first televised presidential debates in the early 1960s between Nixon and Kennedy. As the candidates approached the first debate, Kennedy was asked to put on makeup, straighten his tie and look presidential. His body language reflected his presence and confidence: he made good eye contact with the camera, used appropriate hand gestures to emphasize key points and stood with shoulders squared to the camera. Nixon, however, had just come out of the hospital and was not feeling well. He refused makeup and any type of image consulting at the time. In turn, his shoulders were slouched, he was pale, and his eye contact veered all over the place instead of directly into the camera. Over 80 million viewers tuned in to watch that presidential debate, and of those 80 million, most agreed that Kennedy won the debate, hands down. The audience that did not watch it on television but listened to it on the radio said Nixon won. That inconsistency illustrates the power of body language and appearance. Kennedy looked and acted presidential. Nixon looked ill. Listeners didn't pick up those cues in the vocal expressions, but viewers distinctly noticed the subtle but powerful differences in body language.

In personal branding, you want to ensure that your body language reinforces and supports your positioning and the value proposition (your brand promise) you are promoting to the world. Often, you're not aware of how you are expressing yourself through your physical presence and actions, and you can come across very differently than you intend. Likewise, you can misread other people and make critical decisions simply because of how you interpret their body language.

Effective Body Language Starts with the Face

Have you heard the expression, "If looks could kill"? Maybe you've heard someone say, "He has crazy eyes" or "She has that come-hither look." Facial expressions are the easiest to read and the most revealing of our body language. It has been suggested by communications experts that you should smile when speaking, even if you don't feel like it, because that happy attitude will reflect in your voice. The way you manipulate your face reveals, and sometimes influences, what you're feeling.

Eye Contact

Eye contact is a powerful tool that communicates intent, feelings, and confidence. While animals are instinctively threatened by direct eye contact (if you've ever stared down an animal, you know this), it is a critical element of human communication. People have said the eyes are "the windows to the soul." Thus, it's easy to imagine the kinds of judgments that are made when someone doesn't make good eye contact or averts his eyes often during a conversation. Proper eye contact shows respect, care, trust, and attentiveness. Presenters in front of an audience are often taught to sweep the room with their eyes like a lighthouse beacon because making eye contact with members of an audience is critical to building rapport and gaining trust.

It works the same way sitting across the table from someone. While a person who looks you in the eye shows that he is engaged, focused, and paying attention to you, someone who doesn't make eye contact comes across as disinterested, arrogant, and even superior. If you've ever talked to someone as he is looking over your head or even looking around you for someone else, you understand this perception. In some cases, your dinner companion may have been intimidated or feel nervous about the sense of intimacy that comes with making eye contact. Regardless of the reason, it comes across as, "I'm superior to you and can't be bothered to even look at you."

Eye contact is also a type of intimacy, and becoming aware of the length of time to hold eye contact with a man and with a woman is important. Think appropriateness. If you dart your eyes away too often or your eye contact is too short, you can be perceived as shifty, insecure, or suspicious. If your eye contact is held too long it may appear confrontational or as sexual. When a man holds eye contact too long with a woman, it can be interpreted as an invitation. When he holds eye contact with a man for too long, it can be perceived as threatening (think of "staring someone down"). Likewise, when a woman holds eye contact too long with a man, it can send mixed signals of her intent and credibility. By contrast, when women hold eye contact for long periods with other women, the perception is that she is listening intently. Best practice says that eye contact should last two to three seconds before the other person might become uncomfortable.

The Handshake

In the old days, we shook hands to show somebody we didn't have any weapons. Today, when we shake hands we're creating touch, and touch can offer warmth, intimacy, and personal attention or express anger and intimidation.

When you offer a handshake, make it confident and appropriate. If you've ever shaken hands with someone who gives you a flaccid, weak grip, you know it's not only disturbing but it also conveys judgement about that person. It sends messages of insecurity and reluctance and gives you the idea that he might be hiding something. We tend to perceive the person with the weak handshake as lacking confidence and self-worth. By contrast, a bone-crushing handshake suggests domination, aggression, and an eagerness to compete. When someone takes your hand and squeezes so hard you think your fingers will break, it can be seen as threatening, challenging, and controlling. You want to avoid scenarios where your confidence can be questioned, and you want to project self-assuredness, competency, and self-control with your handshake.

There's an unwritten protocol for the length of time that people shake hands. Hold hands for a moment. Shake hands for a moment. Keep in mind that it's a greeting, a welcoming. See what's appropriate for the situation and circumstances.

Arms and Hands

While volumes have been written about body language related to hands, I'll review just a few tips here. Your hands are capable of conveying many messages. As speakers, for instance, we're taught to show our palms to our audience to build trust and rapport. If I put my hands in my pockets, by contrast, I might appear as if I'm protecting myself; it's a defensive measure. Similarly, if I clench or wring my hands, you could perceive me to be nervous or anxious.

If I put my hands to my face, you might think that I'm being critical and evaluating you. It can also convey insecurity, as if I'm protecting myself. Likewise, if I stroke my chin as you're talking to me, I convey that I'm contemplating or studying something. This is an accepted gesture as long as it is appropriate to the conversation. However, if I start to cover my mouth, especially while I'm talking, I send a message that I want to put the words back in, that somehow I'm not confident in what I'm saying. I would advise you to keep your hands away from your mouth—and your face—altogether, if possible.

Have you ever seen people do a "steepling" gesture, where they tilt the tips of their fingers together as if they're praying? They might believe it sends a message that they are thinking, but it actually conveys the perception that they're perhaps overly confident and maybe even smug. It could appear to others that they are disengaged and judgmental. Be careful with this gesture, unless that is what you intentionally want to communicate.

Similarly, have you ever seen someone put his hands behind his head as if he were stretching and leaning back in his chair? Often, this person will avoid eye contact at the same time. This is a very superior and off-putting posture, especially in a collaborative environment. I witnessed a client do this in a meeting recently when he felt pressured to make a decision on the spot. His body language and posture sent the message to everyone in the room that he would take his time and that decisions were to be made on his schedule. Could he have chosen a more effective way to communicate this? Sure. He didn't need to posture himself in an obvious position of authority, making the other participants in the meeting ill at ease.

We all know what it felt like when our mother wagged her finger or pointed at us as she was talking. It typically meant we had done something she didn't approve of and we were in trouble! You certainly don't want to make others feel like they've done something wrong (if they haven't). If you are an animated personality and talk with your hands, as I do, make sure you show your palms up as much as possible. Use your hands to make a point and let your gestures reinforce and complement what you say, as opposed to detracting and possibly even sending the wrong message. Avoid pointing fingers and instead appropriately use your whole hand pointed forward to emphasize key points in your message, avoiding the military gesture often referred to as "knife hands" or the "NCO point." Your goal is to have your hand gestures support your message not be perceived as overbearing, threatening, or demeaning to others.

We often hear that if people cross their arms, they're defensive or angry. Well, not always. Our most vital organs are in the core of our body and so, yes, there is a defensiveness and protectiveness when we cross our arms if we're feeling threatened. But it is also possible that someone is just cold or relaxed in this position, so be careful about jumping to conclusions when the person you're talking to crosses their arms. Pay attention to the context of the discussion—did you point out a flaw in their work when they crossed their arms? That could indicate insecurity.

What Your Body Language Reveals

- **Confidence**: As a whole, your body language reveals a great deal about you. For instance, confidence is expressed as walking with a wide stride, hands relaxed at your side, shoulders back, and head held high. This stance and posture display self-assuredness. When you are confident, you look engaged (paying attention) and carry yourself with assurance. Confidence and self assurance can enable you to be perceived as open, receptive, and approachable.

- **Approachability** is expressed by having relaxed shoulders and open hands, with palms up and a pleasant expression on your face. When the approachable person walks into a room, he unbuttons his coat to show that he's receptive, that he's present and comfortable. The approachable person faces the person she converses with and has good eye contact. Others see the approachable person as sincere and authentic (doesn't have anything to hide, thus making others feel safe).

- **Defensiveness**: A defensive person, on the other hand, avoids eye contact, might have clenched fists, cross their arms, and turn their mouth down at the corners. The defensive person might chew on their hair or fidget because they feel the need to protect themselves —they're on guard, ready to attack, or defend as needed. If you have a defensive posture, you might constantly put your hands in your pockets or use an object, such as a portfolio or briefcase, to hide behind. All this indicates that the defensive person is insecure about the subject matter or about their position in the room.

- **Anger**: Veterans and civilians, adults and children—we all know what anger looks like. An angry person clenches his fists, wrings his hands, furrows his brow, and even narrows his eyes. He might remain standing (when others sit down) or suddenly stand as if ready to attack. Imagine if you're promoting a personal brand of openness, helpfulness, and warmth and you display these angry gestures. You're not being consistent.

Many people clench their jaws when they're nervous, talking through their teeth with little movement of their lips. You might think it's a way to keep in control, but it comes across as being angry and upset.

- The **frustrated** person paces, wrings her hands, shrugs her shoulders, exhales rapidly, and often over-gestures, as if to compensate and draw attention away from the fact that she's frustrated. She might make too much eye contact, stroke her hair, tap her fingers on a glass or play with a pen or other object. The frustrated person often avoids eye contact as if she were looking over your shoulder for help or a rescue. Watch for this behavior in yourself—you could be sending the message that you are frustrated when you are not.

- **Boredom** creates eyes that wander. The bored person shifts in his seat, yawns, daydreams, and doodles. While drawing or doodling can actually help some people stay focused, so we have to be careful not to always misread doodling as boredom. But if others are doodling and fidgeting and tapping and picking at their nails or hair, it's likely that they're disengaged. When you are in an interview or meeting, check to make sure you are not subconsciously exhibiting this behavior. You could be sending a message that you're bored with the conversation.

- **Lying**: During your military training, I assume you received counsel on detecting untruth from others. It's a critical survival skill to be able to assess whether someone is being truthful or not.

I'm often asked how you can tell when somebody's lying. Studies of polygraph machine results reveal that when we lie, we exhibit emotional arousal and physical changes in the nervous system. We breathe faster and our heart rate and propensity to sweat increases. These are some of the physical responses that the polygraph test is designed to pick up.

In business, most of us are used to watching for physical clues to evaluate someone's honesty. One way a person we might detect lying is when the other person shows us a "fake smile," where she is she smiling with her lips but not with her eyes. Ask yourself, "is her smile inappropriate to the context of our conversation?" If you're talking with a subordinate about financial projections on an assignment and she begins to smile uncontrollably and nervously, this could indicate untruth.

Similarly, no eye contact at all can be a sign that someone is being shifty or deceptive, as discussed earlier. Also, when we're emotionally aroused or stimulated, our pupils dilate, another clue you can use to detect lying.

What you're looking for is incongruity—when the body language doesn't match the message. Is the person shaking her head while saying yes? I learned this from a police officer friend years ago: Often during interrogation, a person will shake her head side to side while communicating an affirmative. The body language does not match the message. Is she fidgeting, licking her lips, or talking too fast? Are his words and body language out of sync? Look for deviations from the norm to assess intent.

Likewise, in our own interactions, we want to make sure we're not communicating with incongruity to our target audiences. We certainly don't want to give anyone the impression we could be lying.

Gender

Gender plays a big role in understanding body language. I've learned that most men transitioning out of the military have not worked closely or often with members of the opposite sex.

In the civilian environment, there are many strict rules around harassment and sexual harassment issues in the workplace. At the same time, understanding the nuances of gender communications and body language are important.

In work relationships, women tend to hold handshakes for a longer time with other women, make personalized eye contact, and nod appreciatively when shaking hands. Men typically shake hands with other men based on their status relationship—peers, boss/staff, colleagues, and salesman/client. The more powerful the man's position, the more aggressive and forceful the handshake might be; often, a firmer, longer, and more abrupt handshake signals higher status.

Men and women also have different tonality and cadence to their speech when talking to each other. Generally, when men talk to men, they tend to drop their voices so they sound more masculine and serious. Women tend to raise their voices when communicating content of which they are nervous or unsure, which can be perceived as apologizing or questioning.

Women also need to watch out for certain subconscious body language messages, such as twirling their hair or playing with jewelry, which have sexual overtones. Men need to pay attention to habits such as jiggling keys in their pockets or fingering cups or pens. Playing with inanimate objects can send the message that you're either nervous, insecure, or bored.

Environmental Factors

What are the conditions in the room? Maybe the room is cold and that's why the person has crossed his arms. In that case, it would be a misperception to assume he's acting defensively. Maybe the room is dark and that's why she's leaning forward and squinting as you speak. She's not being confrontational; she's just having trouble seeing you and hearing you.

Special Circumstances

Various external factors can muddy the context and lead us to the wrong conclusions. For example, it's difficult to accurately read somebody's body language if she's nervous about giving a speech. Likewise, if you've ever seen a speaker get up to give a presentation after the last presenter went long, sometimes the second speaker appears nervous and disheveled when she's just overly conscious of the time. Or maybe she is affected by background noise. Instead of assuming that the presenter is unprepared and not credible, consider the special circumstances as you evaluate her poor body language.

Disabilities

Does the person you're talking to have physical impairments that can be influencing her body language and communications? Is she suffering from a hearing loss? Is he standing on prosthetic legs that might still feel unstable to him? Does he have a nervous disorder? All of these can make a person display a different body language, and we need to take that into consideration.

Spatial Relationships

Americans typically prefer a space difference of about two feet between them and other people. Architects, engineers, and urban developers follow this rule of space when designing buildings, walking paths, and transportation systems. If the room is overly crowded, a person may actually be physically uncomfortable and only appear defensive. If you are talking or standing on a bus or a subway, keep in mind that a person may be uncomfortable because of a proximity issue, rather than with you or the subject matter.

With body language, the goal is to support your personal brand with congruity. Your audience is looking for consistency. When you walk into the room, when I meet you, I want to experience the same person through your body language that I have come to expect when I read your online posts or view your website. I want to see consistency. Only then can I begin to trust that you are who you say you are.

Ask Yourself:

Have I ever received feedback on my body language that was not positive? What was it?

_____

_____

_____

_____

Is the way I carry myself consistent with the values and brand I want to build?

_____

_____

_____

_____

Have I ever sent mixed signals because I wasn't exhibiting consistent body language? What was I doing?

_____

_____

_____

_____

What body language (in others) makes me feel defensive or protective?

_____

_____

_____

_____

What body language (in others) makes me feel welcomed and secure?

_____

_____

_____

_____

Key Takeaways:

- Body language, your own and others', reflects emotions and sends nonverbal cues about how you truly feel.

- Pay attention to your key body language, such as your eye contact and handshakes, and what it can project. You're looking to convey confidence, not superiority, insincerity, or fear.

- Gender differences play an important role in body language. Women and men have very different tolerances and tendencies when dealing with the same sex versus the opposite sex. Take note of these and adjust your actions accordingly.

- Learn to watch for ways you could accidentally be communicating through your body language that you are lying, bored, angry, or frustrated. These could send powerful mixed messages to your audiences and diminish your credibility and impact.

- Body language must always be evaluated in context. Consider environmental and relational factors along with other aspects of the situation as you draw conclusions based on body language cues.

Chapter 24:

Promoting Yourself

Are you comfortable tooting your own horn to others publicly?

Most of the veterans I have worked with have said that self-promotion and self-marketing feels awkward. As we've talked about, the military tends to strip away independence and uniqueness for the sake of safety, consistency, and focus on mission.

This chapter will teach you how to be your own public relations agent and find opportunities and situations where you can publicly self promote yourself with confidence. Here, we will discuss some of the tools you can use to ensure that you have visibility, are recognized for your accomplishments and achievements, and create brand differentiation so that you never compete in a lineup against others who might appear to be like you. Many of you will not encounter the media in your work, nor will you pursue a public profile that gets you in the news. But for those of you interested in using the public relations channel to promote yourself, I offer these suggestions and guidelines to become findable and positioned correctly with audiences who need to know you.

What is PR?

According to the National Public Relations Society of America, "Public relations is a strategic communication process that builds mutually beneficial relationships between organizations and their publics."[15] Public Relations (PR) is how you promote yourself to others and influence a key audience (such as hiring managers, employers, supervisors, colleagues). In creating a PR plan for your personal brand, you will be intentionally building and maintaining your reputation among key audiences through (and with) the media.

Why is Personal PR Important?

A personal public relations plan is similar to a corporate PR plan, starting with strategy and vision and including metrics for success and results. In designing your plan, you might say, "My PR goal is to be approached by ten recruiters that have open jobs in the financial services industry they're looking to fill. That would result in me landing three interviews and one job offer." A PR goal like this, with measurables, gives you something to work towards.

If your personal brand includes being be visible in your industry or being positioned as a subject matter expert (SME) in your field or

---

[15] http://www.prsa.org/AboutPRSA/PublicRelationsDefined

industry, it is helpful to have instances where others (notably the media) have sought your input and advice and referred to your expertise. PR builds "third-party credibility"—when someone credible (an influencer or journalist) writes or reports something about you and audiences believe the information and assign you credibility. To build credibility for your brand, you need key influencers to speak positively about you. You need customers and potential customers, people in the community, and people in your network to speak highly of you. Adding a PR strategy to your personal brand marketing increases the potential influence you can have in your target markets. There are many different components to building your reputation in the marketplace and a number of strategies you can employ.

Media Relations

We often think of public relations as "free advertising" because if you get a newspaper, magazine, or television station to speak about you or interview you, you get publicity without paying for it. PR tells your story in the most competent and confident way, and good PR ensures you'll get fair treatment from reporters. You're positioning yourself as an expert in the marketplace.

Understanding Journalists

Journalists are different from you and me. They serve a broad, diverse, vocal, and highly discriminating audience. Reporters have to be able to explain your story to the general public. They are not interested in fluff. They need information that is valuable and interesting to their readers.

Reporters interested in veteran issues or military in general might find you a valuable resource for comments, insights, and information. While that might serve their purpose, consider whether being a resource on veteran issues serves yours, too.

In PR, it's important to think like a reporter instead of from your own perspective and knowledge level. Here are some important things to keep in mind as you target the media:

- Media relations is not about securing a mutually beneficial relationship. Reporters know you need them more than they need you. Reporters who encounter rude behavior, dishonesty, evasiveness, or even a cancelled interview could blacklist you from their source files. Consider every relationship with a reporter to be a long-term investment.

- Will you lead with your status as a veteran? If you look to secure an interview or place a story about your work or subject matter expertise, consider whether you want to use the veteran angle. Is that germane to the story you are pitching? Are you prepared to answer questions (perhaps on camera, live) that relate to your service?

- Reporters respond best to those who know the scope of their specific jobs. Before speaking with a journalist, consider with whom you'll be speaking. Learn as much as you can about the reporter's background, topics of interest, and audience.

- Newsworthiness is key. Just because you did it doesn't mean its news or that you are in a position to discuss it (remember, some of your military experience is confidential). You need to have something newsworthy to talk about and make yourself relevant to the publication's audience. One way to evaluate the newsworthiness of your story is to answer this question: Who cares? If you can't think of anyone who would care about your story, you'll have a hard time finding a reporter who does. News means news. Reporters are interested in information that's unique, controversial, new, different, and relevant to the largest segment of their audience.

- Reporters look for sources who have track records of honesty, resourcefulness, and accessibility. Reporters try to write balanced stories, which means they may be quoting your critics and competitors as well as your supporters and happy customers. If someone criticizes you and you haven't developed any credibility in the marketplace (if you don't have strong reputation built with your contacts or with journalists in your community), it's likely that a reporter will be skeptical of your side of the story.

- Reporters want sources who have strong brands (reputations) and who may already be known by their audience. This applies to online reputations as well as to the traditional outlets. Is your online reputation invisible? Is it skewed, or is it accurate? Make it easy for reporters to find you and the information and credibility to make you compelling.

- Timing is everything. Reporters love breaking news, firsts, and important new findings! They also want the facts, when they need them—immediately, not tomorrow or next week. Not providing all the pertinent details in time for a deadline can kill the story or your role in the story.

- There are no guarantees. Not only can you (usually) not approve a story before it appears or persuade a publication to print your information verbatim, but your story may not run at all, even after the reporter has given it to his editors. Your compelling and interesting story can be bumped for many reasons: Maybe the reporter found a more appropriate source for the issue, or your story was replaced by a more important or breaking news story. (As noted above, timing is everything.)

- Every "media hit" counts. Many times we don't realize which media have an impact on our business; it's not always the daily newspapers or major TV news outlets. Most people strive for the lead segment on the ten o'clock news, but a hit on the Associated Press wire has a potential for placement in hundreds of papers across the country. Also, although a story in an industry trade publication may look insignificant because you might feel that only your peers will see it and not your clients, there's a snowball effect to consider. Journalists often localize or expand on stories from noncompeting media. They look for trends to illuminate for their mainstream audience by reading trade publications and local news releases. Today's Inside Supply Chain Management story could land on NBC's Nightly News next week or as an article in The Wall Street Journal.

- Media outlets are highly competitive and want to keep their material fresh and original. This means it's unlikely, unless you're Admiral Mullen or President Barack Obama, that you will be featured in more than one competing magazine or TV show around the same time. If you attempt to pitch a story already in the works to a competitive publication, there's a good chance you'll anger all of the media involved.

- Journalists want their stories on the front page, just like you do. Most of them would love to get a great front page, above-the-fold piece that will earn them praise and recognition. Anything you can do to help them achieve that goal will be rewarded with fairness and respect.

A high-ranking military press secretary shared some interesting insights with me about the importance of ALL veterans and active duty military becoming familiar with the do's and don'ts of dealing with the media:

- With the growth of media embeds and online media, be aware that there is a constant barrage of information flowing to the public. This makes it hard for civilians to understand and assess what is real information about war, veteran life, service, and other aspects of combat.

- More so now, members of the Pentagon Press Corps, the White House Press Corps, and other journalists have actual military experience. Many have a national security background, too. This means they will understand terms and situations clearly. It's important to know how to communicate with them.

- Assume journalists want to help and tell the right story to the public but still be on guard.

- Stay in your lane—speak about that which you know well. Unless you are an authority on PTSD, military strategy, or war zone security issues, and are approved to speak on those topics, stick to the issues and areas you are qualified to address.

Preparing for a Media Interview

The reporter calls and wants to interview you! Take the time to get your notes and information in order. It's appropriate to ask the reporter, "What is the general angle of the story?" You're looking to determine why the reporter chose you to be the source—what spurred the idea. Will the interview be live or recorded? Who else is being featured in the story? Try to get as much information as possible about the story ahead of time, and always find out the reporter's deadline.

Also, make sure you know who the reporter's audience is—these are the people to whom you will be speaking.

Making the most of a media opportunity means following five rules:

1. **Always tell the truth.** Personal branding is all about authenticity and transparency, and that couldn't be truer than when dealing with the media. Besides, it is a lot easier to remember one story than many. That said, you don't have to give information you're not comfortable sharing. Remember that your truth may be opinion, so state it as such.

2. **Speak from the audience's point of view.** Anyone who is reading the publication or viewing the broadcast is considering your topic, your story and your company from a "what's in it for me?" perspective. Most people want the conclusion, or the summary, first. Then they'll listen to the supporting information. Before an interview, think to yourself, "What does the audience need to get out of this? What is the headline I want them to write about my interview? What are the three or four important factors in that point of view or position?"

3. **Never reveal confidential information.** With the media there's truly no such thing as "off the record." Never say anything, either before taping a segment or in casual conversation with a reporter, unless you totally and completely trust the reporter. Use your military training here. Be discrete.

4. **Don't feel you have to answer each question you're asked.** As children, we were encouraged to shoot our hand into the air and quickly answer questions asked of us. This is different when dealing with media. Only answer questions you feel comfortable answering, and take your time formulating a response.

5. **Practice in advance.** Repeat your sound bites and rehearse answering them in a succinct and interesting way. Then, imagine the most challenging and ridiculous questions you could be asked. Practice answering those, too.

Leveraging Online Media to Enhance Your Standing with Reporters

Developing an online PR strategy means that you focus on what you want to be known for. What is the reputation that you're creating? What will reporters learn about you online as they investigate whether you're a possible source?

Reporters today admit they rely on social media for sources on areas they are writing about. If you are active and visible and promoting credibility and expertise in your field, chances are reporters will notice you. I have written for several national publications and been featured in others simply because reporters and editors took note of my online activity. From discussions I started on LinkedIn to comments I made on Twitter to my profile as a contributing writer for magazines, I have attracted the attention of notable media. In fact, it is my other work that attracted Military.com, and they asked me to become a regular contributor for veteran transition content. The consistency, commitment, and authenticity I represent online give reporters insight into who I am, what I value, and where I commit my energy and passion.

Ask Yourself:

Can I imagine being in front of the media one day? If so, for what?

_____

_____

_____

_____

How will I communicate my value in a media situation?

_____

_____

_____

_____

How will I "toot my own horn" in my community?

_____

_____

_____

_____

Key Takeaways:

- PR enables you to build credibility for your personal brand by getting others who are seen as reputable sources in the minds of your audience to write or speak about you.

- Consider whether you want to be the veteran media source. Will that positioning help or hurt your ability to get civilian employment? Do you have something unique or insightful to add?

- Effective media relations requires being prepared, authentic, and credible. Talk about what you know, and always be truthful.

- Online social media is as important as traditional media. Don't neglect online journalists, bloggers, social networks, and forums in your PR strategy.

Chapter 25:

Social Media / Social Networking

Whether you are just familiar with social media and social networking or you have been online for years, this chapter will provide unique insight into how you can use the online space to craft your intentional personal brand and broaden your reputation. While I might be very familiar with the strategies and tactics available online, I will focus on how you can use social media to communicate a consistent and intentional message to your target audience.

Social Media vs. Social Networking

Often, we use the terms interchangeably, but they are defined differently. It's important to know the differences because they will drive how you speak to the audiences that you're going to find online.

Social media refers to user-generated content, meaning it has not been vetted. The content is not produced by documented, scrutinized experts in the field but written by any person who happens to think she knows something about a certain topic and publishes something online. It might be in the form of a blog, a micro-blog or a wiki (like Wikipedia, this is a collaboration site for user-generated content not published by vetted experts). Someone might also post something in a discussion forum or comment on an online forum. Social media is also an umbrella term that includes social networking.

Social networking refers to sharing, connecting, and relationship building online. It's very similar to in person networking. You meet people and share information. You decide who you want to be friends with, who you might want to do business with, and which organizations you want to publicly support. Social networking is that part of the social media conversation where you are connecting and sharing.

Social media is an all-encompassing online conversation. You can engage in that and move your personal brand into a position of credibility and relevance by using the right tools, strategy, and methodology. Like any other form of communication and marketing, it should be approached with a strategy in mind. You embark on your personal brand journey to build and manage the reputation you desire, so each piece of the plan requires strategy.

The tools available online to communicate and network are by far some of your most powerful avenues to communicate your brand, strengths, and areas of expertise. Here we'll discuss how to interact online and how to use the variety of social networking tools to find your audience and be found, assuming your target audience is also online. (You would know this after following the steps we discussed in Chapter 16.)

You Can Control the Content

I'm often asked, "Can I control the message in social networking and social media?" Most people believe that the online space is unguarded territory, and they fear a loss of privacy and control if they become active and visible online. Actually, you can control everything you put online. If you write a comment to a blog (or you write your own blog) or post an article online or create an online photo album of family pictures, you're controlling that content.

Similar to the content you post online, you can control with whom you associate online. You can choose your online friends, connections, and the brands you'll attach to through online relationships. Each of those online connections and relationships reflect on your personal brand (by association), which makes it even more important to know with whom you're associating online.

Credibility is King Online

In the online space, credibility is king. To gain visibility and recognition, you must walk the talk of the values you promote. For instance, if you say you are about collaboration, then you must engage in dialogue with others, share resources and celebrate the success of others as well as your own. The online community is extremely transparent, and your contacts will expose an impostor in a very public way. As you build your social network, your goal is to create a real, genuine and engaging online persona that will attract the attention of people who care about issues you care about. Stick to your personal brand plan and you won't go wrong.

Nothing Online is EVER Private.

Today, Twitter posts are being archived by the Library of Congress. Anyone can take a screenshot of a text message, instant message or Facebook post (even if you try to remove it shortly after posting). Don't post anything you wouldn't want your mother and the New York Times to see. Recruiters, employers, colleagues, and your important networking contacts can see anything you type into a screen. When in doubt, don't post/text/share it.

Why Social Media Works

I can tell you, without hesitation, that I have used social media tools to build my international profile. I have written for, and been interviewed by, national magazines because they found me online. I have secured international and local clients because they found me online, saw me positioned as an expert with credibility in various social media or social networking forums, and called.

Whenever a new client or journalist calls and wants to discuss my services and expertise, I always ask where they found me. More often than not, they found me online.

Recruiters are Looking for You Online

Hiring managers, recruiters, and employers routinely look for candidates —and vet job applicants—online. For professional and corporate jobs, they likely look at Google and LinkedIn first. For creative jobs, they might also look at YouTube, Pinterest, and other sites which have a robust visual and social aspect.

Recruiters are evaluating everything from your profile picture, language, content, and connections. They want to see what you have to offer—your experience, skills set, talents, and personality—to the organization. Research by Career Builder and other job boards and websites indicate "41% of hiring managers say they are turned off after seeing references to drugs and alcohol, 40% cite inappropriate images, and 29% point to poor communication skills"[16] and that recruiters are most turned off from candidates who:

- share provocative photos or language (including foul language)

- bad mouth colleagues, supervisors, past supervisors, and others

- display discriminating behavior

- lie about their qualifications

Employers, recruiters, or even your networking contacts will not be privy to inside jokes, slang, or personal bonding between you and your military colleagues. They also may very well not get your jokes. Consider this as you post. Because there is a certain sense of humor and culture in the military (including jargon and language) that doesn't translate to the civilian world, keep private jokes and dialog off your social networks.

---

[16] http://www.foxbusiness.com/personal-finance/2013/10/22/3-things-hiring-managers-dont-want-to-see-on-your-facebook-page/

Consider this insight from a retired Army SPC,

> My Army friends and I were on four different deployment
> rotations (seven months in, seven months out, 90 days in, and
> 90 days out). While any group of us were deployed, there
> would be a group in the rear. We were young, brash veterans
> doing dangerous work, and we weren't exactly in touch or
> forthcoming about our feelings and emotions. Instead of
> saying we missed each other and wishing the other's safety
> (things that would've seemed weak and effete), we invented a
> sort of code. Whenever one of us deployed, every month or so,
> those of us in the rear would get on Facebook and write the
> meanest thing possible on their wall. Things like, "Hey man,
> how are you? I was just thinking about you while I was in bed
> with your wife!" or "Hey, I just wanted to let you know that
> nobody here misses you."
>
> I had some pretty rough days in Iraq and Afghanistan, but
> coming back to see the comments on my wall always made me
> laugh. It was just our way of showing that we missed each
> other.

Things that could be misconstrued or misunderstood, and some points of
pride in the military, are best kept private from civilian professionals.

Pay Attention to Your Friends' Actions

In personal branding, we must pay careful attention to the positioning of
our reputation—our brand—and our image. We should also care about
our associations online. Pay attention to the words and photos posted by

your friends online—their actions will affect your positioning and may reflect your views, simply through your association.

We are often judged by the people we associate with—after all, we chose to be around them. We choose the people we work with, socialize with, network with, and do business with (customers, vendors, colleagues). We are, in part, building our reputation by the people with whom we associate.

This is the message we tell our children: Choose your friends carefully (others will judge you by your friends), don't hang out with the "wrong crowd" (because people will think you make bad choices too), and so on. As adults, however, we often forget this. In social networking, casual conversations, professional relationships, and business partnerships, our associations also directly reflect our values, goals, views, and personal brand. Being conscious and intentional about the message we are sending by the people we collaborate, work, and socialize with is a powerful way to communicate and enhance a personal brand and value proposition.

How to Build Your Personal Brand Online: Start with Google

In evaluating and establishing your online reputation, "ego surfing" or vanity surfing (going to Google or Yahoo, putting your name in quotes and seeing what turns up) will help you determine your existing visibility and social equity (the value of your online presence). You might learn, for example, that something has been posted online about you that is unflattering. You might discover that name is the same as a well-publicized convicted felon. Maybe that's why employers aren't calling you back!

On the other hand, you might find that your online reputation is entirely absent: nothing shows up at all. This could be because you haven't been intentional or focused on your online presence. The good news is that you can fix this!

First, prepare a Google profile by visiting www.Google.com/Profiles. There, you will be prompted to post information about yourself, your career, and your interests. This tool is completely free and tends to rank high in Google searches. A Google profile is similar to a LinkedIn profile where you control the content. Be mindful of the photo and language you use. Take advantage of the Google Profile to make yourself finable to recruiters. Consider it a business tool. If you choose to list your favorite ice cream flavor and politician, then know you can be judged by it.

LinkedIn

Next, I recommend you become active on LinkedIn. When LinkedIn was introduced in 2003, it was where business people went to connect when they were looking for jobs. If your boss found you on LinkedIn back then, it was not a good sign. Today, your potential boss and his boss are on LinkedIn and they're likely looking for you there. Today, LinkedIn is a large, powerful business-networking tool that expands far beyond just job seeking. We use LinkedIn for research, trend analysis, brand enhancement, and networking. As of the writing of this book, LinkedIn is a must for business professionals advancing their personal brands.

LinkedIn is a vast network of people who connect through common interests (in business, industries, discussions), and it highlights the small degrees of separation between people who want to connect. If I have my eye on a potential contact with a large accounting firm that I want to meet, I can look to my network of contacts on LinkedIn to see if any of them know this contact. I simply go into LinkedIn, type the name of my potential contact in the "Search" field, and it shows the names of anyone in my connection network who knows this person, or even knows someone who knows my contact. Suddenly, this potential contact isn't so far out of reach, and an introduction doesn't have to be a cold call. Instead, I can ask someone to whom I am already connected if he could make an introduction for me or offer insight into this prospect, which makes my efforts more successful.

LinkedIn Profile

Your LinkedIn profile (your "page") enables you to start building your online reputation by offering a place for you to write about your professional background, including your specialties, experience, education and interests. Your profile will include your photograph, a description of your experience, and education. From your profile, you will find people who you've worked with in the past, who you've met at networking events, and who you work with currently.

Use your LinkedIn profile to let your personality come through, too. I counseled an Army Sergeant who loved human resources. When he talked about the people side of a business and how organizations benefit from investing in their human capital (skills he learned during his deployment, supported by a Master's Degree he earned after he transitioned out), his eyes lit up. He spoke the language of seasoned human resources professionals and shared a passion for business. We wrote his LinkedIn profile to reflect this enthusiasm and tied his military experience to reinforce his ability to speak a language civilian hiring managers would relate to.

Tips for Building a Powerful LinkedIn Profile:

- **Project a good image.** Use a headshot that shows who you are today. If you use your military photo, in uniform, you could send the message that you have not made the transition fully. Instead, have a photo taken by a photographer or a friend who can use correct lighting and background to show off your personal brand. Be mindful of the background (you won't want images of bars and stores) and choose a setting that is neutral (inside an office) or reflects your passion (for instance, outside with the mountains if you are seeking an outdoors job).

  You should be wearing clothes that also reflect the job you are pursuing. If you seek employment in a corporate or professional setting, you should consider wearing a suit. For a more casual position, a polo shirt and slacks are fine.

  LinkedIn is a business networking site. You will always want to err on the side of being seen as competent, polished, and approachable. That said, your goal will be to demonstrate consistency with your authentic self and your personal brand. This is not the place to project an image of someone who is not you (genuinely).

- **Include a summary**. Include a summary of your experience that does not read like your resume. Resumes are formal and follow a specific structure. On LinkedIn, you can describe your background, interests, goals, and passions in a voice that is more authentic and direct.

- **Use keywords**. LinkedIn is highly searchable. Use specific key words in your summary, title, and experience descriptions that make your profile more findable to prospects, colleagues, and partners. I used several key "tags" or words to make my profile more findable to someone seeking "personal branding," "personal branding for executives," or "reputation management." Under a search (people) for "reputation management" there are over 400,000 results returned. I enjoy my positioning on this list.

- **Update regularly**. Post an update to your LinkedIn status or groups to ensure you stay top of mind with your network. When someone signs up for LinkedIn, they have the option of choosing how often they want to hear from their contacts. Most people opt for once a week or once a day (can be quite a lot). Rarely do people choose not to hear from their network, since the point of LinkedIn is to stay connected. Posting something relevant every 7-10 days increases your odds of being top of mind in the digest of most of your contacts. This average seems to work well for most busy professionals.

Some ideas of things to post: updates on your career progress ("I'm enjoying my work as an intern at Google..."), links to articles, blogs, or news that would interest and inform your network ("This article in the New York Times highlights what I believe to be true about the future of oil drilling studies across the U.S."—with a link to the article), comments or ideas or celebrations about trends, happenings, and topics of interest that relate to your business, industry, or professional circle of influence ("Interesting to see how the state of education is changing as we face a new election cycle..." or "Interesting to see how many veterans are learning to build a powerful personal brand as they transition to a civilian career...").

- **Be genuine.** While LinkedIn doesn't have the social aspects of a network like Facebook, it is still very important to connect with professionals who are genuine and approachable. Showing your authentic enthusiasm, passion, talent, and interests create a well-rounded profile of yourself and what others can expect to experience if they work with you. In the online world of social networking, strive to be authentic in the content you post and comment on, particularly in LinkedIn.

LinkedIn counts executives from all 2013 Fortune 500 companies as members; its corporate talent solutions are used by 91 of the Fortune 100 companies.[17] You can use this tool to reach decision-makers for networking.

When I'm considering executives or companies with whom I want to do business, I research them first on Google and second on LinkedIn. LinkedIn offers a rich professional history on each person listed. It's a

---

[17] http://press.linkedin.com/about

great place to learn more about the person's professional background and to find areas of commonality. When you scroll through someone's LinkedIn profile, you see a wide array of information, which helps you create a positive or negative impression of that person. Recommendations, connections, comments, updates, and job history give you an impression of the type of person you're viewing. Is he well-connected and influential? Is he just starting out in business? Does he share and collaborate with others?

LinkedIn Groups

LinkedIn can also support your in-person professional networking efforts. On LinkedIn, you can join groups that bring like-minded professionals together to discuss important questions and issues within their areas of interest. These can be professional groups, alumni associations, interest groups, etc. Some of these groups also meet in person! For instance, I belong to groups like Leadership Denver, Harvard Business Review, and Forbes Woman. These groups have bulletin boards where members post questions and respond to others' questions. This is an opportunity to engage in a discussion with people from around the globe who share the same business interests or professions.

Avoid a false sense of security in these groups. I participate in some military-to-civilian transition groups to monitor discussions where I can add value or offer insight. On many occasions, I've seen discussions where veterans complain, vent, and air their frustrations with the job search, rant about specific interviewers, etc. Recruiters and employers can see this! Nothing online is ever private. Keep this in mind as you participate in these groups, military or not.

Groups can indicate a person's professional posture. They reflect the companies, topics, issues and areas you are interested in. If you see someone's profile and they show they are active in groups such as Forbes, Harvard Business Review, and the Association for Corporate Growth, for example, your impression is likely that they are involved in business communities around the topic of growth and funding. Join groups with respected publications, industry-leading associations and trade organizations to show engagement with credible voices in an industry.

If, however, you scroll through someone's profile and see they're involved in groups like Weekend Beer Buddies, How to Make Quick Money Without Trying, and Vegas Mavens, you might have a very different impression of the person whose profile you are viewing.

On LinkedIn and other online social media sites where you are posting information for professional positioning, you want to portray a positive impression of your contribution and commitment to the things that are important to you in business and the community. LinkedIn is not the place to share your weekend, political, or religious interests if they do not support the professional image you are working to build intentionally.

Here are some tips I share with clients about using LinkedIn:

- Look for business groups that specifically talk about issues within your industry or profession. If you are a local business, you might choose groups for entrepreneurs, marketers, sales professionals, IT experts, etc. Also, join professional associations in your field, such as the AIA for architects, AICPA for accountants, and so on, and engage in the conversations active in these groups.

- Be careful about having too many military alumni and military-focused groups. Use LinkedIn to keep your military contacts, but if a recruiter sees your profile and they only see military groups and contacts, they might question whether you're truly transitioned and ready to work on the civilian side.

- Show your commitment and connection to your local community by joining the discussion in groups in your area. Look for local business organizations and chambers of commerce, local chapters of national associations, and non-profits involved in business areas you care about. Connect with their groups on LinkedIn and watch for discussions to which you can contribute.

- Reconnect with and promote your past to school alumni associations (almost every college, university, and graduate school has a LinkedIn group online) or previous employer groups. Connecting with your alma mater and alumni groups is a great way to stay in touch with your peers, whether they served in the military or not. I've heard from more than one veteran who reconnected with former classmates who wondered whatever became of them after they enlisted!

LinkedIn groups are a great way to share your expertise, learn from other leaders, ask questions, and bounce ideas off peers around the globe. These discussions build visibility and credibility for you as an expert and participant in a particular industry. Whether you are using LinkedIn for general professional positioning, to find a new job, or to increase your client base, it is critical that people learn more about you online. LinkedIn groups allow you to intentionally create the impression of you that you desire.

LinkedIn "Recommendations"

Recommendations are another valuable asset on LinkedIn. It's important to give and get recommendations. Asking for recommendations can feel uncomfortable, but when done with tact, recommendations will benefit you greatly. Any time I speak at a conference or event or conclude a project with a client and someone says to me, "I'd love to write you a testimonial," I ask him to do it through LinkedIn. LinkedIn recommendations are viewed with such credibility because you can't populate your own recommendations: The only way you can get a recommendation on LinkedIn is for the person writing the testimonial to generate and post it.

LinkedIn lets you review all recommendations made for you before they are published, so you can suggest edits if they are misleading, inappropriate, or out of alignment with your brand focus.

LinkedIn Applications

Similar to Facebook, LinkedIn offers applications you can post on your profile. For instance, you can link to your blog or company's blog so that it feeds recent posts directly to your profile site; you can integrate portfolios of your work and presentations that show off to your expertise; and you can share your reading list directly from Amazon.com to show your interests.

I use LinkedIn to build and augment my professional reputation. I promote my business, the products and services that I offer, and my branding expertise. I list my education and work history but my "Summary" reads more like a bio than a resume. I've received gracious recommendations from clients, partners, etc., and they are all visible to everyone. I also use several plug in (free) applications on my LinkedIn profile and a video that summarizes my business services to help viewers and contacts see how we might work together. On my profile you'll also find recent posts from my blogs, a reading list from Amazon.com, and resources I think are important. I promote my websites and share information that I publish in articles, guest posts, etc.

Facebook

Facebook is another important way to build your online presence. In 2013, there were over 1.19 billion monthly active users on Facebook. Most of them are thirty-five and older, and the fastest-growing Facebook population is forty-five years old. Today, the average Facebook user has over 130 friends.[18] Imagine if you're sharing something important or building a relationship with somebody in your network and they decide to share that information with their network. Your circle of influence is growing and growing!

Use Facebook to bring your brand to life and to humanize yourself to online audiences. I originally joined Facebook at the urging of clients and colleagues who said, "We want to know who you are as a person—your lifestyle, hobbies, family." They wanted to see the human side to my

---

[18] http://newsroom.fb.com/Key-Facts

brand. I took advantage of that opportunity, but at the same time, I control all the content and am very intentional about what I post. The information that you share with others on Facebook is determined by you: You can get as personal as you like, remembering, of course, that your connections will likely expand beyond immediate family and friends. Information such as your birthday (year is optional), your likes and interests, schools, and career history let your personality show through.

Many of you used Facebook to communicate while you were deployed— with fellow troops and with family back home. You posted photos, shared notes, and supported (and received support from) those far away. You celebrated your wins and successes and the memories of those posts are a documentary to your years in service. Now that you are transitioning to a civilian life, you should note what needs to be changed on your Facebook profile. Images, thoughts, and outbursts that might have been acceptable during combat could be frowned upon by a civilian hiring manager if/when they see it. It is important to now make better choices about what to post, what to keep online, and how to engage with others in a public forum like Facebook.

On Facebook, I routinely comment on other people's pictures, posts, and activity. I'm engaged in a dialogue with the people I accept as my "friends." At all times, prior to posting a photo or comment I ask myself, "Is this consistent with how I want to be perceived?" If I'm not one hundred percent sure, I don't post it.

If done well, social sites like Facebook offer a great way to build a personal reputation and credibility within your network of "friends."

Business Pages on Facebook

In addition to a personal profile page, Facebook offers the opportunity to have a page for a business, artist, celebrity, or organization. These pages share information much like a personal profile, and you gather "likes" from followers and fans who want to connect to the page. These pages are public and can be viewed by anyone. When a Facebook user "likes" a page, his network of friends receives that update and can also view and elect to like the page, as well. People who like the page can leave comments on the wall and participate in dialogues, building a collaborative network for the page.

My LIDA360 Facebook business page differs from my personal page in that it focuses exclusively on the business, rather than on me personally. Also, it is open for anyone to "like" and share—anyone can make comments. For this reason, I monitor the page closely to remove spam and any inappropriate content. While I don't directly sell anything on this page, I do promote. I will talk up products that I sell in my online store, upcoming speaking engagements, and other things that I offer. But I also share lots of information on personal branding that is relevant to the people who like this page. I make sure to balance the mix of informing, educating, and promoting.

Consider "liking" pages that offer you:

- Community with, and a way to support, a cause or belief (e.g. financial resources for people of third world countries, fighting cancer, thanking veterans of foreign wars, and so on)

- Connections and contacts with other business professionals (e.g. Chamber of Commerce, local trade associations, etc.)

- Insight, information, inspiration (e.g. Motivational speakers, religious pages, etc.)

- Coupons and offers from your favorite retail brands (many retailers and brands offer their "fans" special incentives and perks as a reward for their online support).

Blogging

Another way to leverage social media and promote your online reputation is to host a blog. If you have a Google profile, a LinkedIn presence, and a Facebook page, a blog could be a natural next step.

A new blog is created every second. With the number of current blogs in the hundreds of millions, I think we could all agree that the term expert is subjective. Technorati, an online publication, reports in its 2010 State of the Blogosphere that sixty-five percent of the bloggers in their study noted that they blog "for fun." The other thirty-five percent were divided among those who blog on behalf of their companies and for themselves as part of a professional effort.[19]

I think blogs are fantastic, if done right. A good blog attracts and retains readers and has a clear and organized focus. In the early days of

---

[19] http://technorati.com/social-media/article/state-of-the-blogosphere-2010-introduction/page-2/

blogging, you could post an online diary of sorts and rant about anything on your mind, and readers would still likely find you. Today, with so many blogs out there, yours needs a defined strategy to stand out.

The most successful (and active) blogs are those that speak with passion and focus and have a unique personal touch. It's important to understand what your readers and potential readers will receive from your blog: Are they looking for humor, education, and information or items of interest or inspiration? Identify a topic or subject area that ignites your passion and energy and is something you are knowledgeable about.

There are many free and low-cost tools and resources available to create engaging blogs. You don't have to be a web developer to build one! WordPress, Blogger, and Typepad are among the biggest platforms out there for free blog hosting. They offer templates that allow you to pick a look and theme that suit you and get right to creating content.

Just like the other social platforms we've discussed, blogging is a dialogue. Even though you publish the content, you want to stimulate a conversation. You should encourage people to comment on your posts and even to link to your blog in their blogs or websites. This increases your blog value and exposure, building your visibility and credibility in the space.

Be sure to blog about things that are consistent with the positioning that you're building. Comment on other people's blogs. Start a conversation. Build a community around a topic.

Blog readers spend one to two minutes reading a post, so you want to make sure that your content is interesting and engaging to your audience. The ideal blog post is 300 to 500 words in length.

Twitter

Initially, I viewed Twitter as too time-consuming, unproductive, and bothersome. Also, I really didn't think I had anything relevant to say to such a broad audience. I quickly learned how to find my target niches on Twitter, build communities of interest, and share information and data with peers and colleagues around the world.

Unlike a blog, which is unlimited in content, Twitter gives you only 140 characters with which to express your point in posts called "tweets." This can be tough! People who are interested in what you have to say can choose to follow you on Twitter. Your tweets are fed through all sorts of RSS (Real Simple Syndication) formats. The tweets by all the people you follow are either fed into a home page that opens when you log into Twitter, into a Twitter application that you can set up to sort and filter your incoming Tweets, or into your mobile device.

I follow quite a few people on Twitter who are on the cutting edge of branding and marketing, and when they post articles or share something, I have access to it. For many people, this makes Twitter a robust RSS feed for news, information, and resources.

Everyone who views your Twitter account can see who you follow (be mindful of this if you follow radical political figures or celebrities who use profanity as their form of communications). As the number of people you follow grows, however, Twitter can start to feel unmanageable, providing dozens of tweets per minute. A number of third-party tools can help filter, organize, and aggregate all this content to keep it manageable. Hootsuite and TweetDeck are two options that allow you to create lists so that tweets on different topics appear in different lists. For example, I follow people who are interested in personal branding in one column. I track my clients in another column so that I can see what they're posting. I track people who are published authors in another column. My followers also put me into lists. I can tell by how I'm listed if my communication on Twitter is accurately portraying my own personal branding, and I check the way I'm listed often. When I see myself listed by others as "Social Media Expert," "Personal Branding," "Public Speaker" or "Marketing Pro," I know I'm on the right track with my reputation on Twitter.

As you transition from service, you might set up lists to follow experts in the field you are pursuing, connect to hiring managers and recruiters at firms you are interested in, or use the filters to follow trends that make you more conversant and knowledgable on business topics.

You can also create keyword search lists on Twitter to see what anyone (even outside those you follow) is saying about a particular topic or keyword. And you can organize tweets to your followers. For example, you can schedule the release of your tweets ahead of time, minimizing the amount of time it takes you to post.

Twitter is a vibrant online community. If I have a question or need advice or resources, I can put it out on Twitter and my followers will respond with information.

If you visit my custom Twitter page, you can see that I have thousands of "followers." These are people who have an interest in what I have to say. I follow people, too. If you've seen my website, you can see that my Twitter page was branded to be consistent with my web page. I use the same photographs, logo, and business description as on my website and other social networking sites. I'm building my brand and my online presence. I'm building consistency.

My strategy for Twitter is to connect with peers, clients, potential clients, and targeted community while building my reputation. I allow some of my personality to come through on Twitter, as I do on all social networking sites. People want to connect with real people. Being human, authentic, and expressive online gives credibility to your personal brand.

YouTube

YouTube has a large presence in our online lives. I was at a football game one night when a scuffle broke out in the stands nearby. Within about two minutes, the number of iPhones and other smart phones that were brought out to capture the event was staggering. When the scuffle was over, several of the spectators said, "This is going on YouTube, baby!"

Now that Google owns YouTube, it is one of the most powerful search engines for content and information. YouTube offers video sharing, information flow, instruction, awareness building, education, and sales. Aside from the videos of stadium brawls, singing dogs, and dancing babies, it can be a powerful tool for you to share advice, demonstrations, tips, hints, and instructions with your target audience.

The beauty of YouTube is the simplicity with which you can share all of this. Let's say you're looking to transition to a career in auto repair, residential real estate, or web design. You can easily produce some quick, one- or two-minute videos on best practices, demonstrations of techniques, or suggestions to help others. You don't have to be a videographer or produce highly formatted edited content. A simple webcam or camcorder is enough to create a video of decent quality.

The ideal video length is under three minutes and viewer attention spans seem to return shorter video search results more quickly.

I have a YouTube presence to share information, educate, and let audiences who may want to hire me see me in action as a speaker. I embed my videos (streamed from YouTube) directly into my website, blogs, and social networking sites. My videos get reviewed and shared on others' blogs as well.

If you use the correct key words and the right tagging on your video, it can certainly increase traffic, draw attention to you, and remove the abstractness of your brand.

The online space is vibrant, fast, and transparent. To be active and compelling online means you start with a strategy for how you will show up, whom you want to connect with (audiences), and a commitment to being a part of a dialog, not just a monologue.

Start engaging with your audience. You might not jump in with both feet, but participate in chat forums and start a dialogue. Have blog interaction with them. Make a commitment to relate with your audience.

They must know you. They have to know where you are, and they have to see you authentically.

Get to Know the Three Types of Online Audiences

Online marketing is about building relationships, and they take time to develop. There are three categories of audiences online: "Zealots," "Influencers," and "Masses."

- **Zealots** are people who are outwardly passionate. Sometimes they're even referred to as "The Passionates." They believe in the cause, the issue, the mission, and they will fight for it until the death. These are great people to attract to the things you feel are important. You can join their movement and eventually become a leader in that movement. Gaining credibility with Zealots opens many possibilities in growing your online credibility. Zealots are obviously a group to pay attention to.

- **Influencers** are probably the hardest group to reach. Influencers started out as Zealots and developed a large following that hangs on every word they say. Influencers have broad reach and tremendous emotional impact on their audiences, but they're skeptical of people who might be selling through them or trying to attach to their credibility for self-serving purposes. Build relationships with the Influencers carefully.

- The **Masses** are the everyday folks. These are people who may not be aware of an issue and aren't actively advocating anything in particular online. They can be enticed and motivated to care, and they could have a large following if properly engaged. With the Masses, your goal will be to gain visibility and motivate them into becoming champions for you and your issues.

Decide How Much Time You Will Spend Online

Social networking can be as time intensive as you want it to be. It is a marketing endeavor, part of your overall communication and networking strategy. The amount of time you spend in social media depends on your strategy. The more (strategic) time you invest, the more rewards you reap.

From a personal branding standpoint, you want to spend about thirty percent of your time focused on marketing to and attracting the attention of the Zealots, the people who have passion and momentum online. Then, focus about ten percent of your time on the people who are influential and have a large following (Influencers). Again, they are hard to get in front of and are often skeptical. They have a lot of credibility at stake.

I recommend you spend most of your time on the Masses, the everyday folks online who align with your target audience. They aren't the well-known names in the industry, but they can become engaged in the conversation in which you're interested in growing your reputation.

Remember To Find Balance

The most important rule to remember for social media is to follow a balance between sharing, informing, asking, and collaborating. Just as you would in person, you want to have a dialogue. It's okay to sell. It's okay to promote yourself. It just can't be all the time. If you were having a conversation in person and immediately started selling, the other person would likely be put off. The online space is no different. Your audience will be open to you selling if you've already built a relationship and offered useful and relevant information.

If you want to be my friend, if you want to be my connection, or if you want me to follow you, I need it to be about me sometimes. It's not all about you, and I want you to celebrate my success, too. When you congratulate me online, with a "bravo" or by sharing news of my success to your audiences, you build your relationship with me.

Seek The Right Venues For Your Audience

There's certainly a plethora of sites that can be applicable for particular audiences and particular strategies. For example, if you own a T-shirt company or if you're a K-12 education company, a lot of your market may be on MySpace or Instagram. If you have an interesting video demonstrating your expertise or your product, you might consider sites like Flickr or YouTube to house the video, since many audiences search online photo and video sharing sites for tutorials. Again, it goes back to starting a conversation with the people who need to find you and doing so where they will be looking for you.

Contribute to Online Publications as Much as Possible

Make sure you reinforce your positioning by contributing often to online publications. Send press releases to online editors. See if you can write for what we call "e-zines," which are online magazines. Consider being a regular guest columnist for an online publication.

Research People Before You Meet Them

Social media offers valuable insights into the people you will encounter online and in person. A quick search through Google or LinkedIn will often reveal if you have something in common before you start the conversation with someone new.

Have Fun and Be Creative

With all the social media available, have fun and be creative. If you prefer to share information with one method over another, use that. Want to create a blog but you don't like to write? How about a video blog? You could post the videos on YouTube, on your own channel, and stream them directly into a blog. Or record your posts and stream them as podcasts if you prefer that to video. Technology continues to get more robust and user-friendly, so let your creativity run free.

If you are new to the online world, don't let that hold you back. Social media is not going away anytime soon. The web offers so many tools and resources for learning about the technical and strategic aspects of these platforms. Each of the sites we discussed has tutorials on its home page. For technical help, YouTube is a great resource with its many how-to videos, as is Ask.com and HowTo.com. For help on how to use more advanced tools and marketing strategies, Hubspot.com, Mashable.com, and ProBlogger.com offer valuable insights and tips in their blogs.

If you take the time to build your initial strategy and let it guide you through your social networking journey, the details will fall into place. Have fun and be yourself.

For most of us, our online profiles are the first place a potential employer, interviewer, or recruiter will go to try to find us. Here are some best practices for using the power of social networking to attract the attention of a future employer:

- **Remember that nothing is private online.** Anything you post in social media (regardless of privacy settings) is public information. Since LinkedIn is a business tool, keep specific client information, project details, and confidential information off your posts and comments. While Facebook is more social, it is still considered "public" regardless of the settings you believe are protecting your privacy. Most posts online are searchable and indexed by Google.

- **Project a positive image.** Look at your headshot and the tone of your profile. Are you projecting an image of someone who is welcoming, approachable, and professional? Are you the kind of job candidate I want to speak with? Or, does the absence of a headshot and the quality of your profile give the impression that you are standoffish and aloof?

- **Use all the available features.** For each social networking site you participate in, use the tools they offer. Most likely, they are there for a reason! For instance, LinkedIn gives you the opportunity to fill out a robust and informative profile. Take advantage of as many of the apps and plug-ins as make sense for you. You might focus on:

  - **Add a summary of your experience in your profile.** Be sure your LinkedIn profile isn't only resume-content. Use the summary to describe who you are and what you do (what are you passionate about?).

  - **Use the Amazon app plug-in to share your favorite books with your connections.** Be sure to include a review of the book and whether you would recommend it to others. This gives your connections more insight into your interests.

  - **Include your past career experience—not as a resume.** What were your successes at that job? What contribution did you make? What did you learn? What did you enjoy the most?

  - **Talk about your military experience in ways that a recruiter or hiring manager will understand.** If you use overly technical jargon and terminology, you might turn off the civilian recruiter. Instead, relate your experiences and skills to understandable values, such as: "Able to make effective decisions quickly.... Understanding of complex engineering systems... Team leader with proven track record for collaboration and effectiveness...." Use civilian language if you are looking for a civilian opportunity.

- **Use targeted keywords.** LinkedIn, Google+, and YouTube are highly searchable. Consider specific key words in your summary, title, and experience descriptions that make your profiles more findable to prospects, colleagues, and partners.

- **Groups.** LinkedIn offers you hundreds of groups to choose from, where you can become engaged and involved in conversations around areas of interest, alumni groups, causes, and business initiatives. Choose the groups wisely—you build your own reputation in part through the groups with whom you associate. Once you join a group, post and comment where appropriate and comfortable. Ask questions, offer insight, and share information around the topic of the group. And, be aware that recruiters and employers watch group conversations, so keep it all relevant and professional.

- **Research.** If your job is landing another opportunity, then you should spend much of your day researching companies, hiring managers, thought leaders, and content in your desired industry and company. There is so much rich information online! Take advantage of the power of Google to learn as much as you can about the industry, company, and people you want to meet.

- **Work it.** If social networking and social media are part of your transition strategy, then treat it as work. Research, share, collaborate, and post insights to ensure you stay relevant. Keep the rants about politics off social networking if you are using this tool

306

for business and career transitioning.

- **Be authentic.** While social networking might feel anonymous and abstract (as opposed to face-to-face meetings), the need is still very strong to connect with people who are genuine and approachable. Showing your authentic enthusiasm, passion, talent, and interests creates a well-rounded profile of yourself and what others can expect to experience if they work with you. In the online world of social networking, strive to be authentic in the content you post and comment on.

Social networking is a vibrant resource for busy people. It affords many tools to build your visibility, share your interests, promote your talents, and connect with like-minded individuals around the globe.

Ask Yourself:

How do I want to appear online (in other words, how do I want to be perceived)?

_____

_____
_____

_____

How will I become more intentional and focused about my online postings, connections, photos, and engagement with others?

_____

_____

How will I remain authentic and genuine online (without getting too personal or inappropriate)?

_____

_____

_____

_____

Who will I seek to network with online?

_____

_____

_____

_____

Key Takeaways:

- Be intentional and strategic in your approach to social media. What is the reputation you're trying to build? Who are you trying to build that with? Where do they hang out online? What do you most want to be known for? If you start with a strategy in mind, it will guide you through all your communication and networking and focus your time and energy toward activity that produces the desired results.

- Take control of your online reputation. Even if you simply start with creating Google and LinkedIn profiles, don't miss out on these basic (and free) tools to promote yourself.

- Strive for consistency in the look, feel, and tone of what you post. If others go to your LinkedIn, Facebook, or Twitter profiles and posts, make sure they see the same person.

- Remember that social media and social networking are about sharing, informing, asking, and collaborating. It is a two-way conversation. Listen and learn from others. Your personal brand will shine as you stay engaged and practice humility.

- Never assume anonymity online. Regardless of the control you feel you have with privacy settings, there are also many ways to get around them. Remember that this is a public space, so only share content that you want to be public.

"The price of success is hard work, dedication to the job at hand, and the determination that whether we win or lose, we have applied the best of ourselves to the task at hand."
--Vince Lombardi

PART IV:

The Job Search

Chapter 26:

Job Search Tools

Throughout this book I've given you the process, insights, and resources to start building your personal brand and become positioned in the most effective way for a civilian career. We have reviewed your current personal brand and your ideal (desired) brand, we've analyzed your target audience and what they need/need to feel from you to make you relevant, and we've walked through numerous marketing tools—from the Elevator Pitch to Social Networking—to bring your value proposition forward.

Here, I will organize those tools and resources for you while you are in the job search. You will need to keep this book close even after you land that first job, because your job after military service will likely not be your last one. You will rely on this process and these tools throughout your career.

The famous business coach and speaker, Zig Ziglar once said, "A lot of people quit looking for work as soon as they find a job." [20] Your career will involve a life-long commitment to constantly improving your skills, options, and value to your employer. Sometimes that will mean changing jobs in order to grow and contribute.

As you move into the civilian job search, you will need some basic tools to be most effective.

Business Cards

As I discussed throughout this book, and particularly in Chapter 21, print business cards for yourself as soon as you have secured a home base and cell phone. You will want your cards to be professional, simple, clear, and reflect your personal brand. The first batch you print does not need to have logos, marks, tag lines, and catch phrases. This is a simple tool that will make it easy for someone you meet to reach you afterwards. Let your other marketing and promotion tools give more details.

Resume

Most likely, you will need to put together a resume to show potential employers the work experience, training, and skills you've gained and to promote your value and relevancy for an open position at their company. There are numerous resume-writing services, online tools, and

---

[20] http://www.brainyquote.com/quotes/quotes/z/zigziglar381978.html

resources available to help you craft an industry-specific or job-focused resume. After you have clarified and established your personal brand, you are in a much better position to investigate those services to ensure your resume is tailored to your reputation and goals. Without personal branding, resumes tend to look generic, unfocused, and lackluster.

In preparing your resume, first focus on content:

- Identify your goals, passion, and value in the "Objective" or "About" section at the top. If you are passionate about systems engineering for the impact it can make to an organization's bottom line and productivity, then state that. Don't assume the reader will see past the words to feel your excitement. Make it obvious.

- Demilitarize your military background to be relevant and understandable. If you were a squadron commander, highlight the responsibilities that entails, the number of troops you led, the budgets you managed, and the results of your leadership. If you ran a combat operation involving heavy artillery and machinery, talk about the skills and talents you brought to the scenario and the technology and people you managed to be successful.

- Identify your experience level, but be aware that it may not come across directly. If you served as a level E-8 or E-9 Sergeant, you may not transition directly to a senior management position in a corporation. There may be some catch up to do. Companies hire and promote based on seniority as well as skill, and even though you had the skills and status in the military, you may be lagging your civilian competitors in areas of corporate culture and business.

As James Rodriguez tells it, "It's important to look at your civilian transition as a career move and not look for a lateral job move. Its unlikely that you'll go from senior military leader to senior business executive in your transition, unless you bring a highly focused skill set in a high-demand industry, such as security or defense."

- Be sure your final resume is complete, free of typos and grammatical errors (have several people proofread it), and polished in appearance. Again, simple and straightforward is preferred over fancy fonts and colorful paper. Your goal is to have your offer come across clearly and authentically. Distractions will only serve to take the reader's eye off the importance of your message.

- Have a few versions of your resume on hand for different scenarios. For online job applications, you might focus one resume to be heavy on relevant keywords to make sure it is searchable and compelling. For corporate resumes, make sure it is brief and focused on results attained. For LinkedIn, you can add more commentary to your resume to show highlights of experience that is meaningful to you.

Always use professional naming for your resume files. Label them "John.Smith_Professional Experience_1" if you need to. Then, keep track of #1, 2, 3 versions so you don't confuse them when you send them to prospective employers. Never title a resume "John.Smith_Resume_focus on IT" as it gives away the fact that you have several focuses.

Cover Letter

You will also have multiple versions of your cover letter to be sent to prospective referrals and hiring managers, along with your resume. Your cover letter should be simple, straightforward, and reflect your image and personality (are you seeing the patterns here?). Leave the fancy paper and fonts aside.

Follow these guidelines for a good cover letter:

- The top of the cover letter should contain: your contact information, the date of the letter, and the address of the recipient (see below).

- The salutation should always be, "Dear Ms. Smith" or "Dear Susan" if she has indicated you may call her by her first name.

- The first paragraph should quickly get to the point of the letter. Indicate the reason you are writing and list the position you are applying for, if you know it.

- Next, outline a couple of examples of how your experience lines up with the requirements of the job. Do not repeat your resume or restate all of your skills, but make it easy for the reader to see that they need to learn more about you.

- While it's important to be authentic and genuine in your cover letter, remember this document serves as a first impression. Instead of showing humor and lightheartedness, demonstrate respect and excitement to indicate you would like to be interviewed for the position. Your personal brand becomes very important in this document. If the position is inside a corporate culture that you cannot fit into, then it might not be worth spending the time trying to bend your cover letter to fit.

- End with a strong close expressing interest in the position and your follow up. Ending with, "I will contact you next week to arrange a time to discuss my qualifications. I look forward to the opportunity to speak with you," takes the burden off the recipient to follow up.

- Send the resume and cover letter as a PDF to ensure the formatting and contents come across in tact.

- Follow up five to seven days after you send the information. Make sure you put a note on your calendar to follow up with this person! Refer to the resume and cover letter you sent and the position for which you are applying. They might not remember you, and that's okay. They likely received a lot of resumes. Following up when you said you would reinforces your interest and desirability as a candidate.

In EXHIBIT D, I share a sample cover letter for you to build off of.

EXHIBIT D:

Jim Smith
4242 Elm Street
Denver, CO 80206
303.555.xxxx
Jim.Smith@host.com

August 8, 2013

Ms. Lida Citroen
LIDA360, LLC
4950 S. Yosemite Street
Suite F2-337
Greenwood Village, CO 80111

Dear Ms. Citroen,

I am writing to express my interest in the Senior Advisor, Technology position you advertised on Monster.com. I understand, from the posting, that you seek a professional who brings exemplary work ethic, skills, ability to work in a fast-paced environment, and an independent thinker. For the past ten years I served as a technical supervisor and IT specialist in the United States Navy and am currently employed as an IT consultant for a financial firm in Colorado. I enjoy the IT field because I see how significant an impact technology, systems, and development are to business efficiency and customer satisfaction.

In my position as an IT specialist in the Navy, I worked closely with our senior command and intelligence divisions to ensure systems operated at optimal levels at all times. In this role, mistakes were costly. I take the responsibility and accountability of my job function very seriously and have been recognized for my commitment, skills, and attitude at work.

To better understand my skills, experience, and interests I am enclosing my resume. I hope you will consider me a strong candidate for this position. I will follow up with you next week to schedule a time to hopefully discuss this position further.

Sincerely,

Jim Smith

Chapter 27:

Positioning Yourself for Success

Positioning yourself as an attractive candidate to a potential employer requires a great deal of time, thought, and effort. As you read through this book, you have hopefully gained ideas and insights about how, where, and when you should be attracting the attention of your target audience.

Previously, I wrote about creating a "pull" strategy for your job candidacy, instead of pushing yourself on every hiring manager with an open position. More and more, recruiters are searching online for applicants, they are asking employees to recommend friends and colleagues for open positions, and they are networking with other recruiters to find outstanding candidates in the market. Being positioned for success means you are the person these people think of when looking to fill a position that you would want.

Remember to position yourself for success in person by using these tools:

- Focus on building an intentional network of contacts. Refer back to Chapter 20, and make sure your contact database contains decision makers, information sources, and cheerleaders.

- Show up authentically as you meet new contacts. Let them experience your brand and talents through actions, not just words. Focus on your image, body language, and tone when you meet new people. First impressions matter!

- Build credibility by telling people what you believe in and what you value. Make sure you "walk the talk" and have action to support your values.

- Give as much, or more, than you take. Be on the lookout for how you can help someone else and be a resource for them.

- Position yourself as a subject matter expert or valuable connection by providing insights, information, connections, and advice in your industry.

- Be that person others want to help. Sincerity, trust, and authenticity go far in building relationships with people.

- Online positioning offers you a great deal of exposure and connections, with little cost. Be sure to create a well thought out LinkedIn profile using the tips and strategies we discussed in Chapter 25. Be sure to make connections, accept connections, and build networks based on your professional goals and the opportunities you desire. LinkedIn is a business tool, not the place friends hang out and share war stories. Keep it professional.

Remember to stay top-of-mind relevant with your LinkedIn network. Update your status, comment in groups, and send congratulations notes to your contacts to show that you're active and engaged. Post links to articles, information, and content along with a note that offers insight from you.

- Follow blogs, discussion boards, and industry and news sites that your target audience is watching and participating with. As you post comments, opinions, and insights onto these boards and forums, you will get the attention of the people who might be looking to hire.

- Google yourself regularly or set up a Google Alert so you are notified when your name appears online. Be sure to quickly catch any negative or misleading posts or information about someone with your same name before a hiring manager does. Then, take steps to fix the post or repair your online profile with the tools we discussed in Chapter 25.

Chapter 28:

Research and Preparation

Preparing for the job search (as well as the interview) requires research. You will likely do much of your research online, although talking to people in the industry and who might know your target companies is also very helpful. The more you can know before a phone or in-person interview, the better. Knowledge is power!

When you identify a company you would like to pursue or you've been called for an interview, start by looking online:

- Research the company/organization. Look through their website and any online reviews you can find. Check out sites like GlassDoor.com to see how employees express feelings about the company. Make sure you understand their core business, industry, and target audience. Make a list of questions to clarify anything you don't understand about the company, such as, "Where does the company see the market growing in the next 5 years?" or "How will the changes to federal funding impact the company's ability to diversify services going forward?" Questions are a great way to show you have done research and are focused on the future of the company.

- Google the hiring managers and recruiters or look up their LinkedIn profiles. Do you have any areas of common interest or experience? Do they list military service or have a passion for working with veterans? Do you share any contacts?

- Check www.Hoovers.com or the Better Business Bureau (www.BBB.org) to see if there have been complaints, issues, or legal actions filed. This could indicate an environment you don't want to pursue.

- Check the company's LinkedIn company page to see if you know anyone who is connected. Then, go to your own network of LinkedIn contacts and check to see if anyone you know worked for this company or knows someone who does.

- In person, follow up with those people you know (through networking, casually, or on LinkedIn) and ask for an informational meeting to learn:

  - What is the culture at that company like? Do employees enjoy working there and stay long term? Is there high turnover?

  - What growth or challenges has the company experienced? Are they stable or struggling?

- What community activities does the company promote? Maybe you can meet a company recruiter at a fundraiser in your area.

- What does the company value in its employees? Does the company tend to hire "win at all costs" types or does it support a strong work ethic and integrity with employees?

- Have notes and questions ready from this research. Identify what areas of the company, its business, culture, or mission you need more clarity on and be prepared to ask the interviewer for more information.

Chapter 29:

The Interview

"During the interview in which I landed my current position, I implemented the techniques I learned from Lida. In doing so, I was able to convey trust and confidence in my current chain of command that I would be able to assimilate into the corporate environment, be proactive in learning the business, and use initiative to improve standard processes and procedures. I believe that marketing myself in this manner led to my full time offer because it took much of the mystery out of who I was and what I was capable of doing, despite not having any corporate work experience." — Greg L.

Great! You got the call! You have the interview! Before you head out the door be sure you are prepared and will show up as authentic, focused, and compelling to the hiring manager.

Messaging

As you prepare for the call, consider:

- What attracted you to the job you're applying for?

- What about your background, skills, and brand make you the ideal candidate?

Review your elevator pitch and brand promise. Practice your elevator pitch in front of a mirror or friend if it has been a while since you last shared it.

Remind yourself to demilitarize your background to make your experience relatable by a civilian hiring manager. Keep the graphic details and jargon out of your responses.

Review standard candidate interview questions and your responses. For instance, the question, "Tell me about yourself," is not an invitation to relay your life story. This question is designed to see how well you relate your background to the needs and goals of the company in hiring for the open position. This is where your personal branding is critical! Consider these questions, as well:

- What do you know about our company? (This is where your research will be critical.)

- What does your ideal workday look like? (Be able to describe how you like to work: with other people? independently? solving problems or implementing solutions?)

- Have you ever had a situation where there was conflict with a supervisor? How did you handle it? (They want to see your ability to articulate the situation—without emotion—and how you played an active role in fixing conflict.)

- What would your past colleagues say about you? (Here is a great personal branding question!)

- What are your outside interests? (Do not talk about things that are potentially offensive or disturbing. Stick to hobbies like running, camping, reading adventure novels, and travel.)

- What stresses you? (The interviewer knows that everyone has stress. To say "nothing" is not truthful. Identify areas that you are stressed—when others don't live up to their word; gossip; or offering negative feedback to peers could be acceptable responses.)

Image

- Make sure you are dressed in an appropriate fashion for the nature of the meeting. Interviews are generally formal and hiring managers expect to meet someone dressed in a suit and tie (women in conservative dress or suit). The interviewee shows respect by "dressing up" even if the hiring manager is not formally dressed.

- Check that your shoes are polished and the soles are in tact (no holes).

- Fingernails, hair, and face should all be clean and groomed.

- Pop a breath mint into your mouth as you leave for the interview. Make sure you don't have gum or mints in your mouth when you get to the interview.

Bring to the Interview:

- Clean copies of your resume, even if you have emailed it to the interviewer. Print copies of your resume on quality paper, and be sure they are free of smudges, creases, and dirt.

- Business cards with your name, email, and cell phone number on them.

- A pad for note taking (plain, lined paper, with no logos on it). Have your questions neatly written on this pad.

- Pen to take notes with (again, stay free of logos or pens that light up).

- A portfolio to carry your resume, note pad, and pen. Most portfolios have a slot for business cards—keep your stack separate from the one the interviewer may hand you. And, remove other people's card from your portfolio before you leave for the interview. If you can't get a portfolio, put your notepad and resumes in a file folder to protect them.

"It is difficult to make a man miserable while he feels worthy of himself and claims kindred to the great God who made him."
-- Abraham Lincoln

Chapter 30:

Closing Thoughts

I felt a great deal of responsibility in writing this book. I believe it is an honor and obligation of mine to share my learnings, resources, and tools with each of you as a sign of appreciation for your service to our country. Your sacrifices ensure that I am able to have the liberties and freedom to do what I love for a living, in a beautiful and safe place.

I congratulate you for being open to the personal brand process and starting your journey. Being able to promote yourself and build your reputation is simple in methodology, but it is not easy! Likely, as you've read this book, there have been parts or sections you've struggled with, either emotionally or tactically and other parts that came naturally. The beauty of personal branding is that it is highly individual: No two clients of mine have been the same. They have their own unique goals, values, issues, challenges, and desired opportunities.

When I wrote my first book, *Reputation 360: Creating power through personal branding* (Palisades Publishing, 2011), I wanted to make the message and personal branding tools accessible to anyone, wherever they were. I envisioned executives reading the book as they tried to become more relevant to their clients. I pictured stay-at-home moms and college graduates using the tips to position themselves with confidence as they face a tough job market. And I wrote the book for the administrative assistant, construction worker, bus driver, and PhD who wants to create more meaning and connection to their work and mission in life.

This book was written specifically for you, the veteran transitioning from a military career to a civilian one. Some of you have come back from service very different from how you left. Injuries, PTSD, brain trauma, and psychological distress are real to you and require that you overcome many more obstacles than those of us who have not experienced your sacrifice.

This book has laid out many of the tools, ideas, tips, and examples to illustrate the road to building a credible reputation. Having a defined and compelling personal brand takes effort and time; it's not something that can be thrown together in a pinch. The first step is always the hardest.

In working with veterans over the years, I have worked with TOPGUN pilots, Naval submarine commanders, Green Berets—veterans across all branches of the United States Armed Forces. Each time I've met a veteran, I'm struck by the hesitation they share about the transition to this next (civilian) chapter in their life. Most of them tell me they feel ill-prepared and apprehensive about what lies on the "civilian side" and how they can position themselves most effectively.

332

My wish is that your transition can be smooth, intentional, focused, and productive. I wish that you won't encounter too many roadblocks and obstacles from civilian employers who mean well but do not know how to receive you and your talents into the organization. My dream is that you will find your passion, calling, and value in the world outside the military with the same dedication and satisfaction that made you successful in your service to this country.

By clearly defining who you are, how you want to be known, and how you plan to live up to that brand promise every day, you put yourself in the best seat to drive your next career. You will attract desirable opportunities because your decisions and actions are intentional. A clearly defined brand will help you thrive in your career in these ways:

- **Gaining credibility.** Credibility is built when you actively communicate what you stand for and then act accordingly. If you say you're open and approachable but no one can ever get in touch with you, you lose credibility. Likewise, if your door remains open but you don't communicate that value of openness, you may not get credit or recognition for being open. Building your personal brand helps you understand and then act on the values you want to project to the world, making it easier to establish credibility.

- **Staying ahead of the competition.** What is it that makes you unique and valuable in your position? It's your personal brand. Skills and knowledge can be found elsewhere, but how you do your work—how you build relationships, solve problems creatively, and bring teams together to collaborate—cannot be outsourced or easily replaced. These factors secure your value to your clients or employer because you bring something to the table that no one else does.

- **Opening yourself up to personal growth.** The process of personal branding requires that you periodically measure the distance between your current brand and your desired reputation. It's a process that helps you see your strengths and weaknesses with clear vision and helpful insight. Using feedback and other tools, you'll strengthen the assets that make you unique and address the weaknesses that may hold you back.

- **Strengthening your connections.** Creating an intentional brand is not something you do in a vacuum. It requires that you create an intentional network of people with whom you share knowledge, support, ideas, and even leads. When you put thought and effort into building a network that gives and takes and connects, your brand becomes stronger and more valuable—and more meaningful!

- **Improving career advancement.** Putting intention and strategy behind your actions will break you out of the day-to-day rut and help align your efforts with your goals. It will give you purpose and keep you motivated. These are the pieces that work together to advance your career and help you create the life and legacy that you want. It doesn't happen overnight, and it's never too soon to take control of your reputation and make sure you're heading down the path that you want most.

- **Live an authentic life.** By understanding your passions, interests, values, and goals, you can affect your future in new and exciting ways. Many civilians struggle with the same concepts you are now

334

being introduced to—how to be more intentional and genuine in designing your career and happiness. Living authentically means that you will focus on doing work that is meaningful and important to you, make choices that are right for you (and maybe not other people), and be accountable to yourself to be happy.

I have been fortunate to work with some of the most influential, committed, and passionate individuals in the corporate and non-profit environments around the world. What they have in common is a strong desire to be in control of their future, to own their reputation, create the legacy they desire, and be recognized for their contribution. Just like you.

I have also met, collaborated, and worked with some of the most forward-thinking and inspiring veteran advocates this country has seen. From visionaries like General Peter Pace who started Wall Street Warfighters Foundation to John Melia, who founded a group to serve the needs of returning wounded war veterans (Wounded Warrior Project) to Dan Goldenberg, who is impacting the veteran community through his work at The Call of Duty Endowment, ensuring veterans groups receive resources to meet the growing needs of this population.

One of my friends and colleagues, Dana Niemela, provided inspiring testimony at her Colorado Senate Confirmation Hearing for the State Board of Veterans Affairs, 2013. Here is an excerpt from her speech:

> *My name is Dana Louise Niemela. I was commissioned as an officer in the United States Navy out of the ROTC program at The George Washington University in Washington DC. I started my career in aviation in the 1990s, in the years following Tailhook and Kara Hultgreen, who many of you may not know. Suffice it to say, it was a particularly interesting time for women to be in the aviation field, particularly those of us who were interested in combat*

aviation. Well, as it turned out flying off aircraft carriers was not in the cards for me and that working in logistics would be the most amazing opportunity I could have ever imagined for myself.

I served the Commander of the Sixth Fleet in the Mediterranean from 2000-2002, onboard the USS LaSalle. In those two years we saw the attack on the USS Cole and the terrorist attacks of September 11th, 2001. We saw our mission shift dramatically from one of foreign diplomacy to one of national defense and all the things that come along with that. And even though, yes, I volunteered to join the United States Military, I could never have imagined myself standing watch on a pier in a foreign country, with a loaded weapon at my fingertips, ready to fire, if that was what was necessary to protect the men and women onboard that ship. I was 26 years old.

In 2002, two weeks after I left the USS LaSalle to serve the Chairman of the Joint Chiefs of Staff, the Leading Petty Officer in my division on board the LaSalle was killed in an accident. While I grieved his death, I also felt tremendous guilt for not being there for my sailors when they need support and leadership the most. I had to go about my daily business as if nothing were wrong. And my daily business was not the norm. I witnessed the Chairman of the Joint Chiefs of Staff, first-hand, making the agonizing decisions that come with sending our troops to war. At that time, I was also serving the President of the United States at the White House. And when it came time for me to leave the military, by choice... well, you couldn't have paid me to believe what that was going to be like.

I spent the next five years working in corporate America, flying completely under the radar. I had too many conversations with people who thought that my military service opened the door for anyone and everyone to share their opinions about the wars. I had close friends, shipmates, serving in Iraq and Afghanistan, and they had families at home and were putting their lives on the line daily to defend our freedoms. In the meantime, my American neighbors were going about their everyday lives, with their yellow ribbon on their bumpers and acting as if nothing were happening. The focus of conversations was always what was happening on The Jersey Shore or what Paris Hilton was wearing. So I felt it prudent to keep my mouth shut. There were people with whom I worked for five years who never knew I served for eight years in the military. It was a part of me better kept secret.

I tell you this because it's relevant. My service was "normal." I did not see combat. I did not spend 12-18 months in Iraq or Afghanistan, thousands of miles away from my family and my children, getting shot at and seeing my friends die around me. I didn't go back, three or four times before I was 28 years old. I had what many would call a very "vanilla" eight years of active duty, and I struggled. I didn't know how I fit in. I was sad. I was disoriented. And I didn't know what to do about it.

After five years, it was a retired Marine Corps Master Gunnery Sergeant who finally snapped some sense into me. He asked, "What's your problem, Lieutenant?! You served. You're a veteran. Get over it. Now DO something." You see, it takes a vet to understand a vet and to give us the motivation we need to take action. And so, Master Guns, I am doing something.

I've had the opportunity to tell my story to countless women veterans, student veterans, and homeless veterans. What I have found is that my story is important. My words have an impact. I help those who are struggling with the same things I did, and much, much worse, get engaged and on the right track. I am the voice that veterans need, particularly those who feel they have no voice.

And while that is all good work, it's not good enough.

Our political and social climate is veteran-friendly in a way we haven't seen in generations, but it's not good enough. As long as women veterans are feeling the need to remain anonymous, I have not done enough. As long as veteran unemployment is higher than that of the rest of society, I have not done enough. As long as our veterans are sleeping in the streets and struggling to meet the basic needs of their children, I have not done enough. As long as our brothers and sisters, our sons and daughters, are coming home to their own war and killing themselves, I have not done enough.

WE have not done enough.

In closing, I'd like to share the words of a fellow sailor, John Paul Jones, and tell you that "I have not yet begun to fight." And I look forward to fighting, alongside all of you, for the men and women who have fought for us. Thank you.

This book was intended to inspire and ignite your personal brand power and create the blueprint for you to design a strategy and game plan that is right for you, personally. I look forward to hearing your feedback, reviews, questions, and successes at www.LIDA360.com.

Stay Informed and Engaged

I encourage you to continue learning and discovering about your personal brand by joining our conversation online. Sign up for additional tools, updates, and an online continuing discussion about veteran transition needs at www.YourNextMissionBook.com. I will post new information, videos, and resources for you on a regular basis. Continue your personal brand journey well into your transition.

"I don't measure a man's success by how high he climbs, but how high he bounces when he hits bottom."
— George S. Patton

About the Author

Lida Citroën is an international branding and reputation management specialist who designs and enhances the identities of companies, executives, and thought-leaders globally. As principal and founder of LIDA360, LLC, Lida is a sought-after expert in the field of brand development, reputation management, and online marketing, leveraging a comprehensive go-to-market perspective and incorporating clients' business objectives to create an authentic brand experience.

Lida is passionate about helping veterans transition from military service to civilian careers. She is an active member of ESGR (Employer Support of the Guard and Reserve) where she helps employers understand how and why to hire veterans. She continues to travel to Philadelphia to volunteer her program to the Wall Street Warfighters Foundation, which trains veterans for careers in financial services. A regular contributing writer to Military.com, Lida speaks nationally at conferences and events focused on the veteran transition.

Recognized for her expertise and experience in personal branding and reputation management, Lida is often featured in the media, including: Fortune Magazine, Forbes.com, Harvard Business Review, ICOSA

Magazine, Kiplinger's Personal Finance, KUSA 9News, Fox31 News, and ColoradoBiz Magazine.

Lida is the author of *Reputation 360: Creating power through personal branding* (Palisades Publishing, 2011), a best-selling guide for civilian professionals looking to gain competitive advantage through reputation management.

On the corporate side, Lida is an accomplished speaker, engaging audiences with her empowering message about intentionally managing your personal brand and reputation to achieve career success. She regularly presents workshops, keynotes, and presentations on reputation management, branding, image, and using social media to international companies and organizations, helping their employees build a personal brand that supports the business.

While she loves to travel and explore the world, Lida enjoys her home base in Greenwood Village, Colorado, where she spends time with her husband, sons, two Golden Retrievers, and a very overweight cat.

Lida can be contacted at www.LIDA360.com or www.YourNextMissionBook.com.

CPSIA information can be obtained at www.ICGtesting.com
Printed in the USA
LVOW08s0924201114

414702LV00001B/1/P

9 780983 169048